DISCOVER
Second Grade
Math & Language Arts

Beginning Sounds

Look at each picture below...
with. Then...

Name That Pattern!

...ach pattern using letters.

Thinking Kids™
Carson-Dellosa Publishing LLC
Greensboro, North Carolina

MW00607214

Thinking Kids™
Carson-Dellosa Publishing LLC
P.O. Box 35665
Greensboro, NC 27425 USA

Printed in the USA • All rights reserved.
01-177157811

ISBN 978-1-4838-1671-5

Table of Contents

© Carson-Dellosa
CD-704891

Introduction

Welcome to *Discover Second Grade!* This book contains everything you and your child need for a creative approach to math and language arts practice. It gives you the tools to help fill knowledge gaps and build foundations that will prepare your child for higher-level math and language arts. Your child will learn to think about, know, apply, and reason with math and language arts concepts.

Discover Second Grade is organized into nine sections based on the skills covered. Each activity supports the current state standards and offers a fun and active approach to essential second grade math and language arts skills. Creative and open-ended lessons build a concrete example of math and language arts concepts to help promote understanding.

This book aims to increase critical thinking and problem solving skills with colorful and entertaining activities. Each activity supports early learning standards and encourages children to connect with the essential math and language arts skills they are learning. Activities call for children to draw, use tally marks, pictures, and graphic organizers. The goal is to encourage students to show different ways to answer questions.

Each activity challenges your child's critical thinking and problem solving skills. In *Discover Second Grade,* your child will learn about:

• Numbers and Operations
• Algebra
• Geometry
• Measurement
• Data Analysis and Probability
• Reading
• Reading Comprehension
• English
• Spelling

Add each pair of numbers by breaking the second number into tens and ones. Then, add the groups of ten and add the ones. The first two have been started for you.

$56 + 23 =$

⬇

$56 + 20 + 3 =$

⬇

$76 + 3 =$

⬇

_____

$28 + 14 =$

⬇

$28 + 10 + 4 =$

⬇

_____ + _____ =

⬇

_____

$46 + 39 =$

⬇

_____ + _____ + _____ =

⬇

_____ + _____ =

⬇

_____

$32 + 17 =$

⬇

_____ + _____ + _____ =

⬇

_____ + _____ =

⬇

_____

Addition Breakdown

Add each pair of numbers by breaking the second number into tens and ones. Then, add the groups of ten and add the ones. The first two have been started for you.

57 + 33 =

⬇

57 + 30 + 3 =

⬇

87 + 3 =

⬇

_____

---

25 + 13 =

⬇

25 + 10 + 3 =

⬇

_____ + _____ =

⬇

_____

---

48 + 34 =

⬇

_____ + _____ + _____ =

⬇

_____ + _____ =

⬇

_____

---

37 + 18 =

⬇

_____ + _____ + _____ =

⬇

_____ + _____ =

⬇

_____

Mystery Numbers

Use tally marks to help you find the missing number behind each magnifying lens. Write a number sentence to solve for the missing number. Then, write the answer.

77 – 🔍 = 70

_____ ☐ _____ = _____

🔍 = _____

29 – 🔍 = 17

_____ ☐ _____ = _____

🔍 = _____

Mystery Numbers

Use tally marks to help you find the missing number behind each magnifying lens. Write a number sentence to solve for the missing number. Then, write the answer.

$21 - $ 🔍 $ = 10$

_____ ▢ _____ = _____

🔍 = _____

$37 - $ 🔍 $ = 15$

_____ ▢ _____ = _____

🔍 = _____

Use the hundred board to solve each problem. Circle the first number in the problem on the board. Then, draw a path on the board as you count back to subtract the second number. Draw a triangle around the answer. Write the answer to complete the number sentence.

22 – 11 = _____   67 – 14 = _____   36 – 9 = _____

88 – 12 = _____   94 – 5 = _____   51 – 12 = _____

1	2	3	4	5	6	7	8	9	10
11	12	13	14	15	16	17	18	19	20
21	22	23	24	25	26	27	28	29	30
31	32	33	34	35	36	37	38	39	40
41	42	43	44	45	46	47	48	49	50
51	52	53	54	55	56	57	58	59	60
61	62	63	64	65	66	67	68	69	70
71	72	73	74	75	76	77	78	79	80
81	82	83	84	85	86	87	88	89	90
91	92	93	94	95	96	97	98	99	100

Square Subtraction

Use the hundred board to solve each problem. Circle the first number in the problem on the board. Then, draw a path on the board as you count back to subtract the second number. Draw a triangle around the answer. Write the answer to complete the number sentence.

31 – 10 = _____   57 – 13 = _____   19 – 8 = _____

77 – 12 = _____   99 – 6 = _____   88 – 10 = _____

1	2	3	4	5	6	7	8	9	10
11	12	13	14	15	16	17	18	19	20
21	22	23	24	25	26	27	28	29	30
31	32	33	34	35	36	37	38	39	40
41	42	43	44	45	46	47	48	49	50
51	52	53	54	55	56	57	58	59	60
61	62	63	64	65	66	67	68	69	70
71	72	73	74	75	76	77	78	79	80
81	82	83	84	85	86	87	88	89	90
91	92	93	94	95	96	97	98	99	100

Count the dots on each side of each domino. Then, write the related facts for each domino.

_____ + _____ = _____

_____ + _____ = _____

_____ − _____ = _____

_____ − _____ = _____

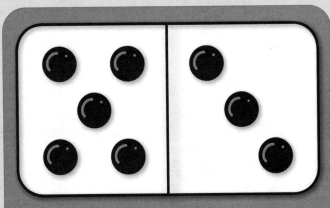

_____ + _____ = _____

_____ + _____ = _____

_____ − _____ = _____

_____ − _____ = _____

Dip into Dominoes

Count the dots on each side of each domino. Then, write the related facts for each domino.

____ + ____ = ____

____ + ____ = ____

____ - ____ = ____

____ - ____ = ____

____ + ____ = ____

____ + ____ = ____

____ - ____ = ____

____ - ____ = ____

Elevator Operator

Look at the first and last numbers in each number sentence. Did the first number go up or down to become the last number? Circle the correct elevator button beside the number sentence. Write + or – in the blank to make the sentence true.

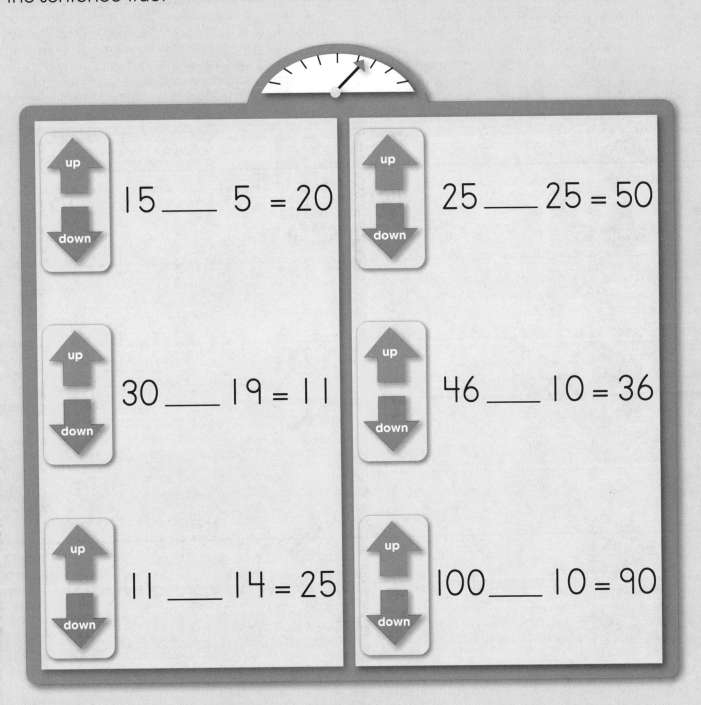

15 ___ 5 = 20

25 ___ 25 = 50

30 ___ 19 = 11

46 ___ 10 = 36

11 ___ 14 = 25

100 ___ 10 = 90

© Carson-Dellosa
CD-704891

Elevator Operator

Look at the first and last numbers in each number sentence. Did the first number go up or down to become the last number? Circle the correct elevator button beside the number sentence. Write + or – in the blank to make the sentence true.

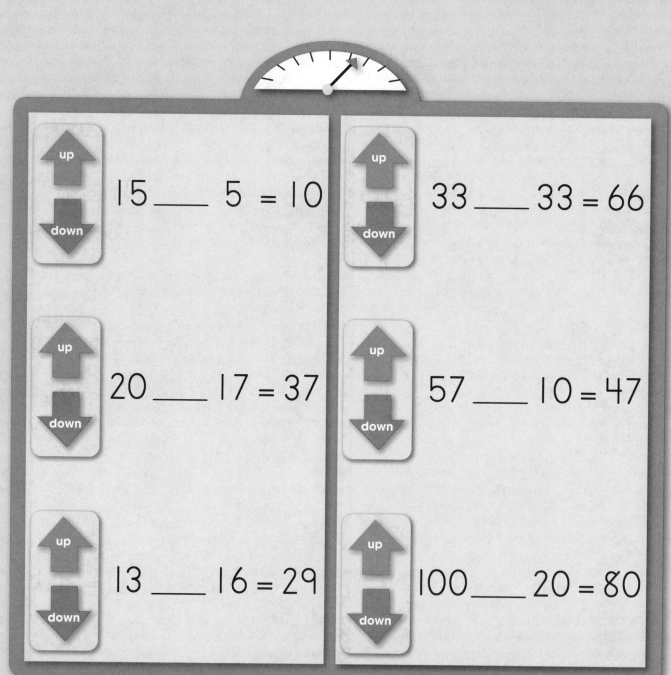

up
down
$15 \_\_\_ 5 = 10$

up
down
$33 \_\_\_ 33 = 66$

up
down
$20 \_\_\_ 17 = 37$

up
down
$57 \_\_\_ 10 = 47$

up
down
$13 \_\_\_ 16 = 29$

up
down
$100 \_\_\_ 20 = 80$

Hopping on a Number Line

Use the number line to help you write multiplication sentences and answer the questions.

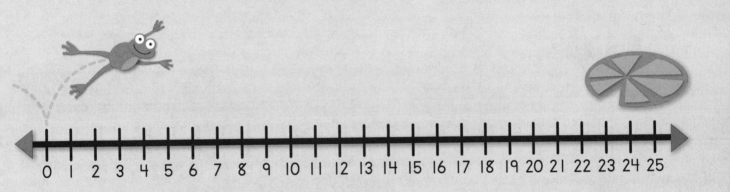

If the frog takes 5 hops of 3, where will he land?

5 × 3 = _____

If the frog takes 6 hops of 2, where will he land?

_____ × _____ = _____

If the frog takes 4 hops of 4, where will he land?

_____ × _____ = _____

If the frog takes 3 hops of 7, where will he land?

_____ × _____ = _____

Hopping on a Number Line

Use the number line to help you write multiplication sentences and answer the questions.

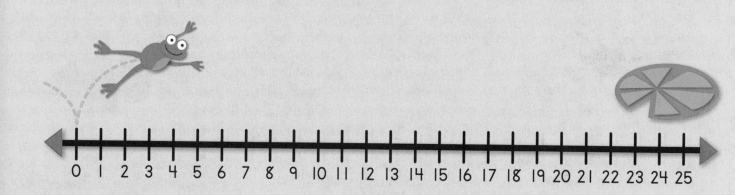

If the frog takes 5 hops of 2, where will he land?

$5 \times 2 =$ _____

If the frog takes 6 hops of 3, where will he land?

_____ $\times$ _____ = _____

If the frog takes 3 hops of 3, where will he land?

_____ $\times$ _____ = _____

If the frog takes 4 hops of 6, where will he land?

_____ $\times$ _____ = _____

Fruitful Arrays

Count the fruit in each array. Write two number sentences to describe each array. In the last box, draw your own array and write two number sentences to describe it.

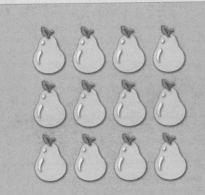

___ + ___ + ___ = ___

___ × ___ = ___

___ + ___ = ___

___ × ___ = ___

___ + ___ + ___ = ___

___ × ___ = ___

Fruitful Arrays

Count the fruit in each array. Write two number sentences to describe each array. In the last box, draw your own array and write two number sentences to describe it.

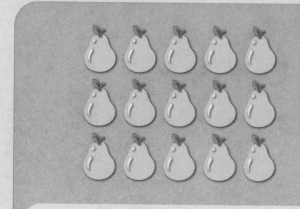

____ + ____ + ____ = ____

____ × ____ = ____

____ + ____ = ____

____ × ____ = ____

____ + ____ + ____ = ____

____ × ____ = ____

Discover Second Grade

The Great Divide

Show 4 ways that you can divide 20 pennies into equal groups. Draw each way on a planet.

Share and Share Alike

Rachel has treats to share with her 3 dogs. Circle 3 equal groups in each jar. Complete the sentences. Then, write a division number sentence and solve.

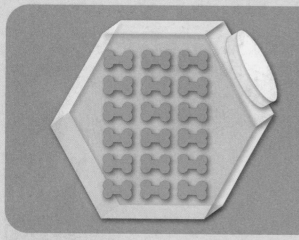

Three dogs shared _____ bones.

Each dog ate _____ bones.

_____ ÷ _____ = _____

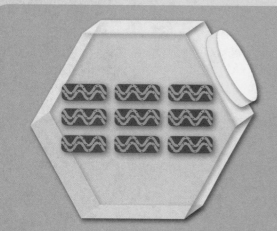

Three dogs shared _____ strips.

Each dog ate _____ strips.

_____ ÷ _____ = _____

Three dogs shared _____ cookies.

Each dog ate _____ cookies.

_____ ÷ _____ = _____

Share and Share Alike

Jim has treats to share with his 4 dogs. Circle 4 equal groups in each jar. Complete the sentences. Then, write a division number sentence and solve.

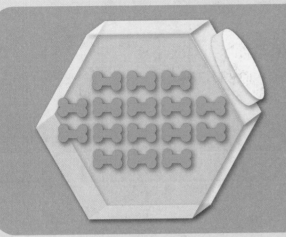

Four dogs shared _____ bones.

Each dog ate _____ bones.

_____ ÷ _____ = _____

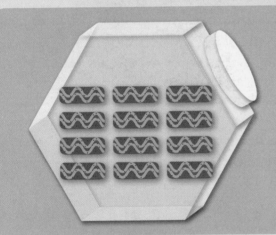

Four dogs shared _____ strips.

Each dog ate _____ strips.

_____ ÷ _____ = _____

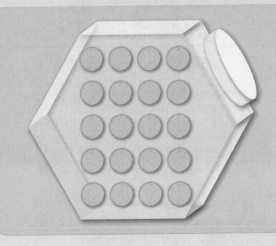

Four dogs shared _____ cookies.

Each dog ate _____ cookies.

_____ ÷ _____ = _____

What Should You Do?

Read each word problem. Draw a picture or an array to solve each problem. Write the number sentence.

There are 36 books on 4 shelves. Each shelf has the same number of books on it. How many books are on each shelf?

_____ ▢ _____ = _____ books

There are 8 baskets. Each basket has 5 apples in it. How many apples are there in all?

_____ ▢ _____ = _____ apples

What Should You Do?

Read each word problem. Draw a picture or an array to solve each problem. Write the number sentence.

Logan is paying for himself and 3 friends to go to the movies. The tickets cost $7 each. How much money does he need?

_____ _____ = $ _____

A clown at a party has 24 balloons. There are 6 children at the party. How many balloons will each child get?

_____ _____ = _____ balloons

Double Duos

Use doubles addition facts to find each sum.

5 + 5 = _____   3 + 4 = _____

Think:
3 + 3 + 1

9 + 9 = _____   6 + 7 = _____

Think:
6 + 6 + 1

2 + 2 = _____   4 + 5 = _____

Think:
4 + 4 + 1

7 + 7 = _____   8 + 9 = _____

Think:
8 + 8 + 1

Double Duos

Use doubles addition facts to find each sum.

4 + 4 = _____   2 + 3 = _____   **Think:**
                                         2 + 2 + 1

8 + 8 = _____   7 + 8 = _____   **Think:**
                                         7 + 7 + 1

3 + 3 = _____   1 + 2 = _____   **Think:**
                                         1 + 1 + 1

6 + 6 = _____   5 + 6 = _____   **Think:**
                                         5 + 5 + 1

Take the Shortcut

Use the shortcuts to find each difference.

− 8 **Shortcut**	− 9 **Shortcut**
Think: −10, +2	**Think:** −10, +1

14 − 8   ___ − 10 + 2 = ___

30 − 9   ___ − 10 + 1 = ___

20 − 8   ___ − 10 + ___ = ___

40 − 9   ___ − 10 + ___ = ___

Discover Second Grade

Use the shortcuts to find each difference.

– 8 Shortcut
Think: –10, +2

– 9 Shortcut
Think: –10, +1

13 – 8

___ – 10 + 2 = ___

20 – 9

___ – 10 + 1 = ___

30 – 8

___ – 10 + ___ = ___

50 – 9

___ – 10 + ___ = ___

You have $1.00. Estimate to find out if you have enough money to buy the items listed. Use coins to check your answers. Then, circle yes or no.

Do you have enough to buy a yo-yo and a top?

yes   no

Do you have enough to buy a toy train and a toy sailboat?

yes   no

Do you have enough to buy a ball and a teddy bear?

yes   no

Do you have enough to buy a pencil and a toy sailboat?

yes   no

You have $1.25. Estimate to find out if you have enough money to buy the items listed. Use coins to check your answers. Then, circle yes or no.

Do you have enough to buy a toy train and a pencil?

yes   **no**

Do you have enough to buy a toy train and a yo-yo?

yes   **no**

Do you have enough to buy a ball and a toy sailboat?

yes   **no**

Do you have enough to buy a pencil and a yo-yo?

yes   **no**

Brain Power

Use mental math to find each sum. (Hint: Make tens or multiples of 10 first.) Then, write in the cloud how you solved each problem.

12 + 5 + 8 + 5 =

31 + 7 + 3 =

7 + 9 + 13 =

80 + 19 + 1 =

Brain Power

Use mental math to find each sum. (Hint: Make tens or multiples of 10 first.)
Then, write in the cloud how you solved each problem.

13 + 4 + 7 + 4 =

41 + 8 + 2 =

8 + 7 + 14 =

70 + 18 + 3 =

The Speed Machine

Use a calculator to solve each problem.

84 + 56 = _____

93 – 47 = _____

36 + 19 + 55 = _____

703 – 284 = _____

563 + 459 = _____

1,001 – 699 = _____

Use a calculator to solve each problem.

$85 + 66 =$ _____

$92 - 44 =$ _____

$34 + 18 + 56 =$ _____

$707 - 167 =$ _____

$571 + 455 =$ _____

$1,010 - 688 =$ _____

Clothing Sort

Sort and classify the clothing into groups. Then, on a separate sheet of paper, write how you classified each group.

Look at the shapes in each row. Name the sorting rule for each group. Follow the directions to show 3 shape blocks that do not fit the rule. Then, draw the shapes.

Rule: _____   Show 3 blocks that would break the rule.

Rule: _____   Show 3 blocks that would break the rule.

Rule: _____   Show 3 blocks that would break the rule.

Color the blank beads to continue each pattern.

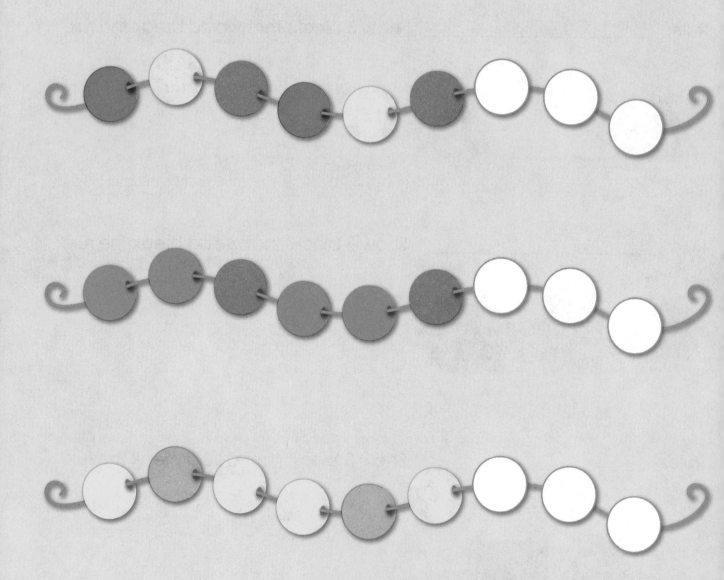

Bead a Pattern

Color the blank beads to continue each pattern.

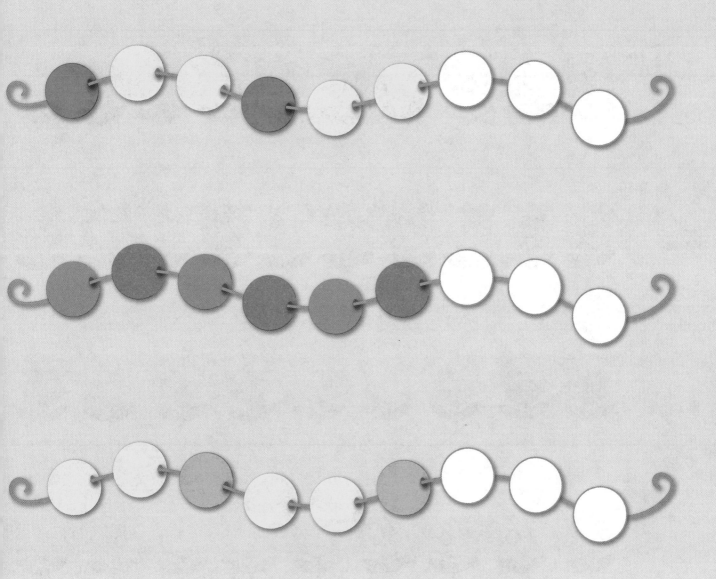

Buzzing Around

Write the missing numbers in each row of flowers.

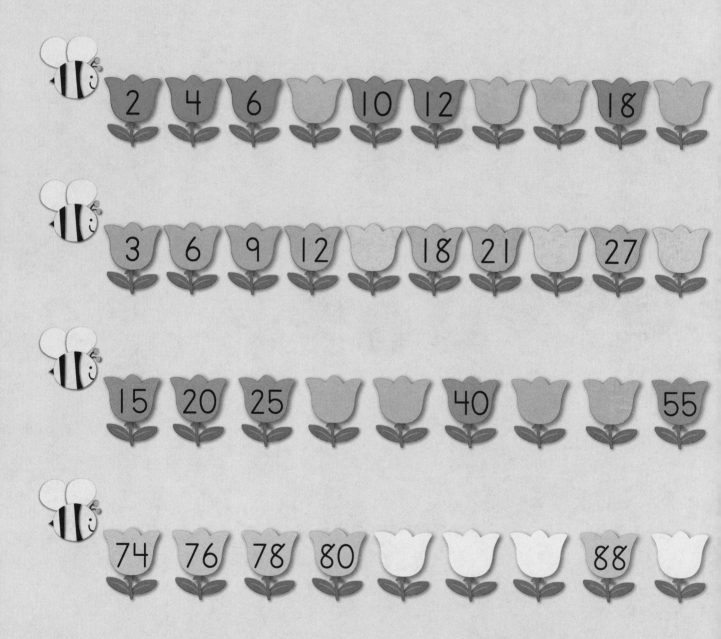

Row 1: 2, 4, 6, ___, 10, 12, ___, ___, 18, ___

Row 2: 3, 6, 9, 12, ___, 18, 21, ___, 27, ___

Row 3: 15, 20, 25, ___, ___, 40, ___, ___, 55

Row 4: 74, 76, 78, 80, ___, ___, ___, 88, ___

Write the missing numbers in each row of flowers.

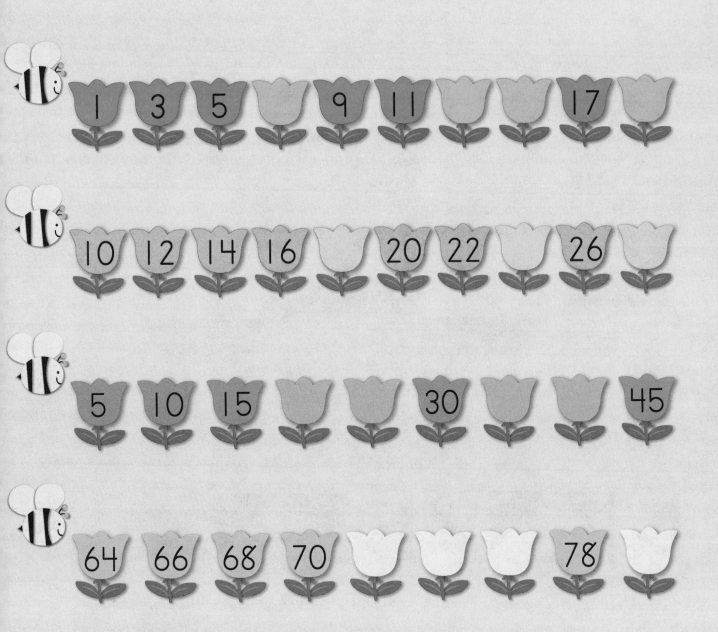

Row 1: 1, 3, 5, __, 9, 11, __, __, 17, __

Row 2: 10, 12, 14, 16, __, 20, 22, __, 26, __

Row 3: 5, 10, 15, __, __, 30, __, __, 45

Row 4: 64, 66, 68, 70, __, __, __, 78, __

© Carson-Dellosa
CD-704891

What Comes Next?

Draw the shape that comes next in each pattern. Tell whether the shape was slid, turned, or flipped.

Look at the rules and number patterns. Write the missing rules and numbers.

Rule: +7 ⭐ 14 ⭐ ⭐ ⭐ ⭐ ⭐ ⭐

Rule:____ 19 17 15 13 11 ⭐ 7 ⭐

Rule: −3 ⭐ ⭐ 22 ⭐ ⭐ ⭐ ⭐ ⭐

Rule:____ 85 80 75 ⭐ ⭐ 60 55 ⭐

Out of This World Patterns

Look at the rules and number patterns. Write the missing rules and numbers.

Rule: +6 ★ 14 ★ ★ ★ ★ ★ ★

Rule: ___ 63 59 55 51 47 ★ 39 ★

Rule: −5 ★ ★ 65 ★ ★ ★ ★ ★ ★

Rule: ___ 44 47 50 ★ ★ 59 62 ★

Name That Pattern!

Name each pattern using letters.

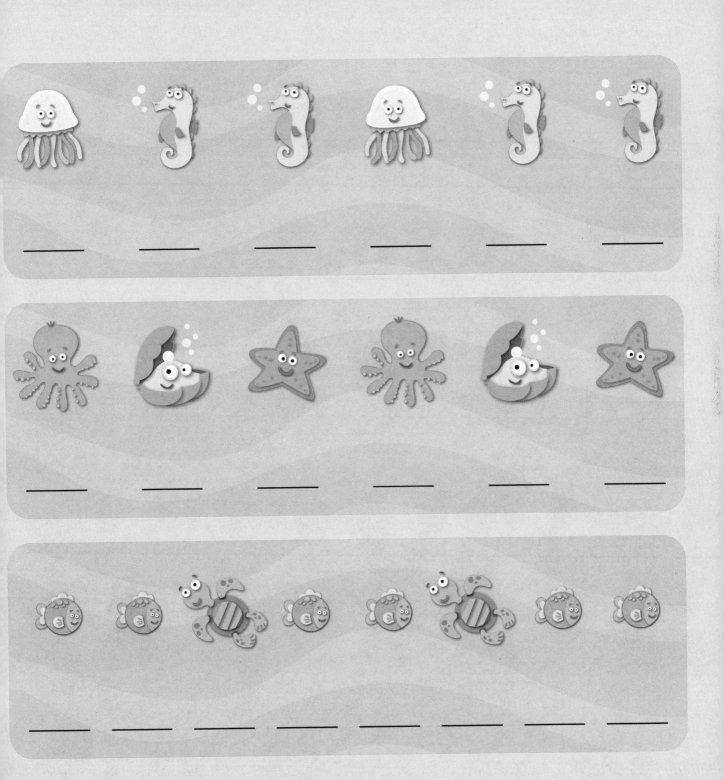

___ ___ ___ ___ ___ ___

___ ___ ___ ___ ___ ___

___ ___ ___ ___ ___ ___ ___ ___

Name That Pattern!

Name each pattern using letters.

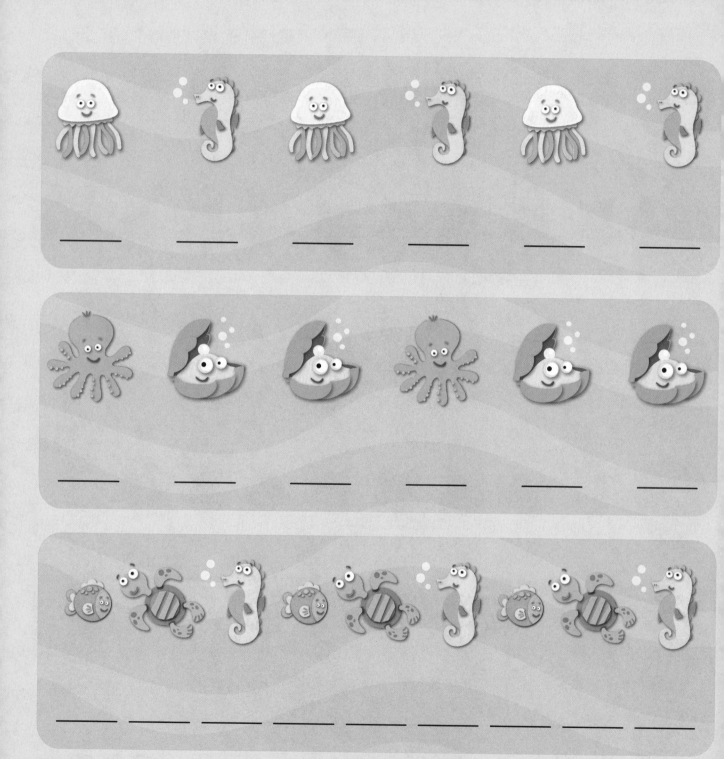

___ ___ ___ ___ ___ ___

___ ___ ___ ___ ___ ___

___ ___ ___ ___ ___ ___ ___ ___ ___

Puppy Patterns

Name each pattern using letters. Then, draw circles and squares to copy the pattern.

Clap, snap, or tap each pattern.

Name each pattern using letters. Circle the repeating parts in each letter pattern. Then, create a matching pattern by drawing circles and squares.

_____ _____ _____ _____ _____ _____ _____ _____ _____

_____ _____ _____ _____ _____ _____ _____ _____

What Repeats?

Name each pattern using letters. Circle the repeating parts in each letter pattern. Then, create a matching pattern by drawing circles and squares.

___ ___ ___ ___ ___ ___ ___ ___ ___

___ ___ ___ ___ ___ ___ ___ ___ ___

Bucket of Buttons

Each child named the button pattern in a different way. Explain each child's rule.

A B C A B C A B C

Explain Jayla's rule: _____

A B A A B A A B A

Explain Carson's rule: _____

A A B A A B A A B

Explain Nina's rule: _____

What's the Rule?

Draw what comes next in each pattern.

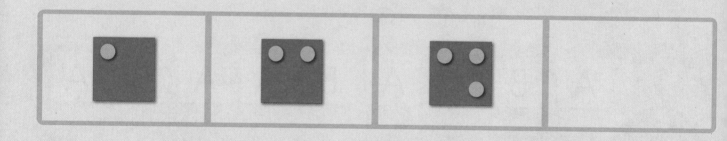

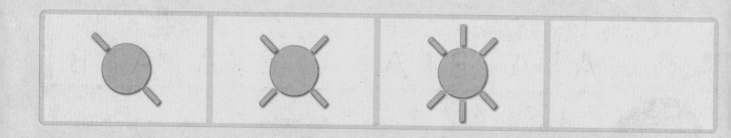

Draw what comes next in each pattern.

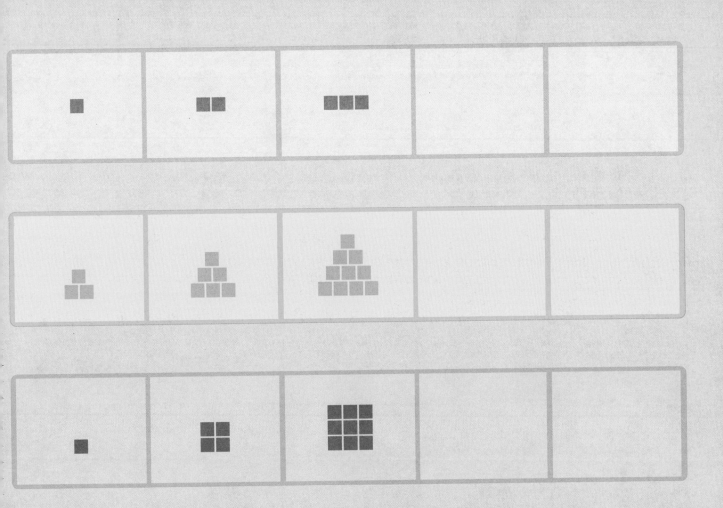

Missing Pieces

Draw the missing sets in each pattern.

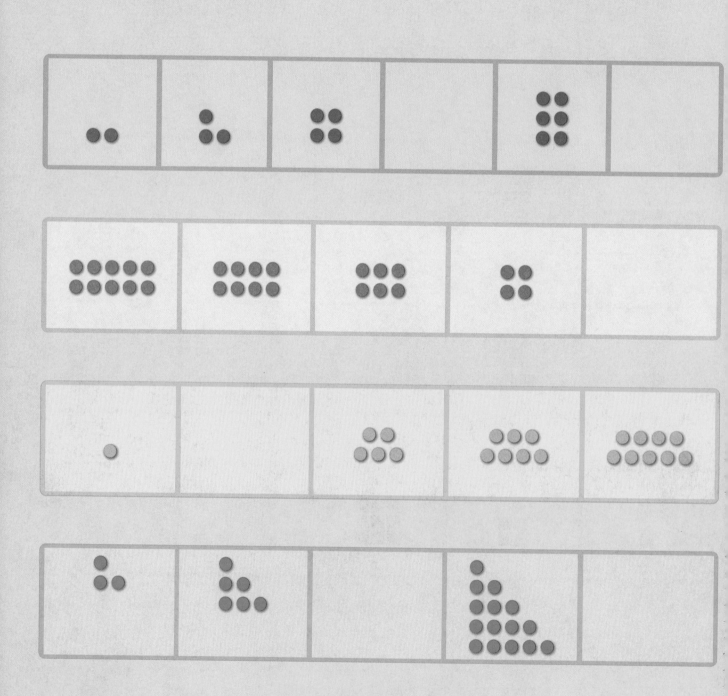

True or False?

Decide if each statement is true or false. Circle T for true or F for false.

If 3 + 4 = 7, then 4 + 3 = 7.　　　　T　　F

If 20 + 0 = 20, then 0 + 20 = 20.　　T　　F

If 3 + 4 + 4 + 2 = 13, then
13 = 2 + 4 + 4 + 3.　　　　　　T　　F

If 12 − 0 = 12, then 0 − 12 = 12.　　T　　F

If 23 + 50 = 73, then 73 = 50 + 23.　T　　F

If 18 − 9 = 9, then 9 = 9 − 18.　　T　　F

True or False?

Decide if each statement is true or false. Circle T for true or F for false.

If $3 + 5 = 8$, then $5 + 3 = 8$.   T   F

If $30 + 0 = 30$, then $0 + 30 = 30$.   T   F

If $2 + 3 + 3 + 5 = 13$, then
$13 = 5 + 3 + 3 + 2$.   T   F

If $13 - 0 = 13$, then $0 - 13 = 13$.   T   F

If $33 + 60 = 93$, then $93 = 60 + 33$.   T   F

If $17 - 8 = 9$, then $17 - 9 = 8$.   T   F

Figure out the missing number behind each picture. Then, write the number.

$40 + $ ⬤ $ = 50$

⬤ $ = $ _____

🍃 $- 70 = 20$

🍃 $ = $ _____

$10 + $ ⭐ $ = 30$

⭐ $ = $ _____

$80 - $ 🎈 $ = 20$

🎈 $ = $ _____

Figure out the missing number behind each picture. Then, write the number.

$$30 + \bigcirc = 70$$

$$\bigcirc = \underline{\hspace{2cm}}$$

$$\text{🍃} - 60 = 30$$

$$\text{🍃} = \underline{\hspace{2cm}}$$

$$20 + \bigstar = 40$$

$$\bigstar = \underline{\hspace{2cm}}$$

$$90 - \text{🎈} = 60$$

$$\text{🎈} = \underline{\hspace{2cm}}$$

Write >, <, or = in each circle to make each statement true.

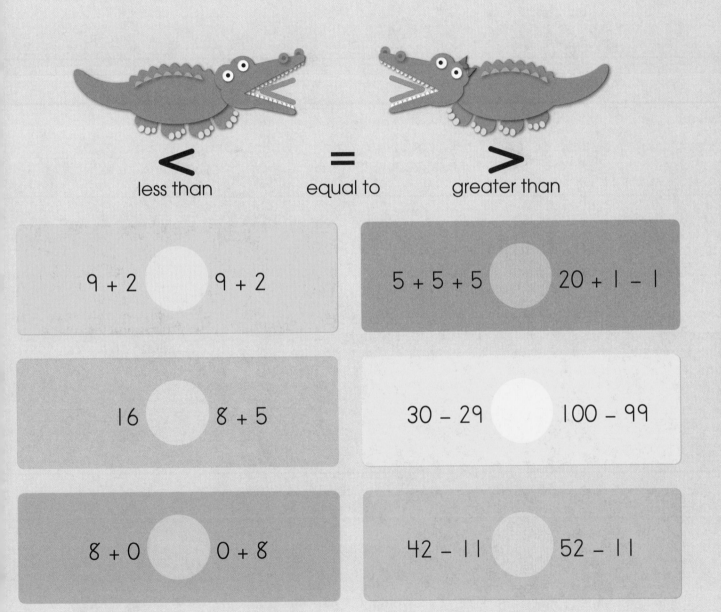

< less than   = equal to   > greater than

9 + 2 ◯ 9 + 2

5 + 5 + 5 ◯ 20 + 1 − 1

16 ◯ 8 + 5

30 − 29 ◯ 100 − 99

8 + 0 ◯ 0 + 8

42 − 11 ◯ 52 − 11

Write >, <, or = in each circle to make each statement true.

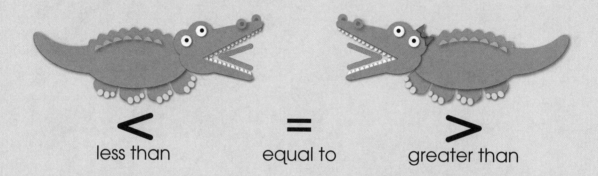

< less than   **=** equal to   **>** greater than

8 + 1 ◯ 10 + 11	6 + 6 + 6 ◯ 20 – 1 – 1
17 ◯ 8 + 9	60 – 59 ◯ 99 – 98
9 + 0 ◯ 0 + 9	33 – 11 ◯ 44 – 11

Mystery Machines

Write the missing numbers and rules for each machine.

Machine 1

IN	OUT
8	18
24	34
	43
17	
61	

RULE: _____

Machine 2

IN	OUT
100	95
	49
17	12
99	
	0

RULE: _____

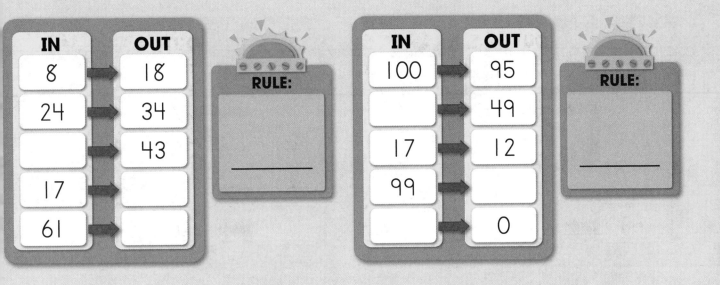

Machine 3

IN	OUT
84	
	19
4	
46	
	12

RULE: −3

Machine 4

IN	OUT
21	
14	
	35
1	
	63

RULE: +7

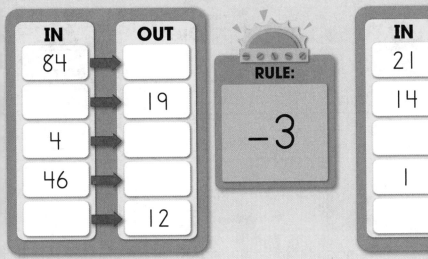
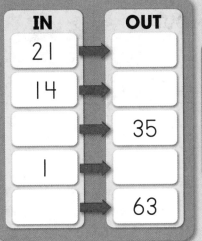

© Carson-Dellosa
CD-704891

Mystery Machines

Write the missing numbers and rules for each machine.

IN	OUT
9	17
22	30
	33
16	
69	

RULE:
_____

IN	OUT
100	94
	27
41	35
67	
	0

RULE:
_____

IN	OUT
88	
	17
6	
42	
	13

RULE:
−2

IN	OUT
31	
83	
	62
1	
	23

RULE:
+5

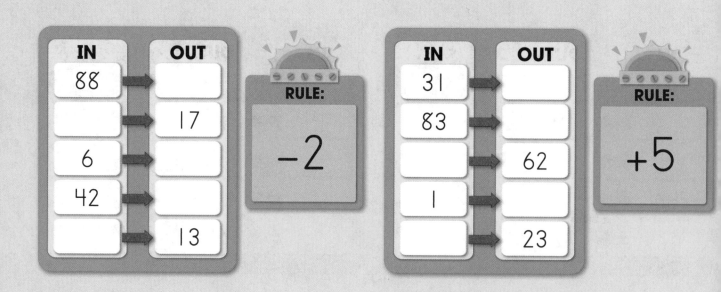

Follow the rules in each box. Write the missing number on each object.

Rules: = + 4 = – 2

1 2

Rules:  = + 10 = – 20

1 0 0

Rules: = + 3 = – 1

1 8

Count Up and Back

Follow the rules in each box. Write the missing number on each object.

Rules: = + 5   = − 1

12

Rules:  = + 11   = − 22

100

Rules: = + 6   = − 4

18

© Carson-Dellosa
CD-704891

What's the Weather?

Read the temperatures on Monday's weather map. Then, read the temperatures on Tuesday's weather map. Write the temperatures for each city. Then, record the difference in temperature for each city.

Monday

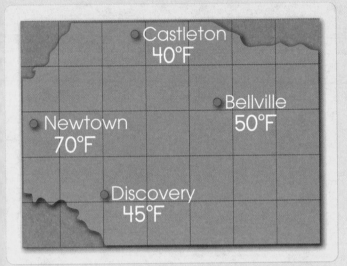

Castleton
40°F

Bellville
50°F

Newtown
70°F

Discovery
45°F

Tuesday

Castleton
45°F

Bellville
65°F

Newtown
80°F

Discovery
50°F

	Monday	Tuesday	Difference
Castleton	_____ °F	_____ °F	_____ °F
Newtown	_____ °F	_____ °F	_____ °F
Bellville	_____ °F	_____ °F	_____ °F
Discovery	_____ °F	_____ °F	_____ °F

What's the Weather?

Read the temperatures on Friday's weather map. Then, read the temperatures on Saturday's weather map. Write the temperatures for each city. Then, record the difference in temperature for each city.

Friday

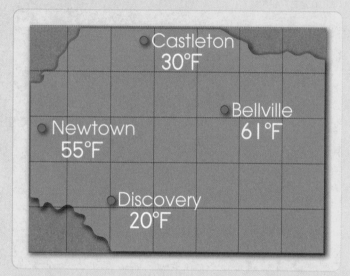

Castleton
30°F

Bellville
61°F

Newtown
55°F

Discovery
20°F

Saturday

Castleton
33°F

Bellville
47°F

Newtown
58°F

Discovery
15°F

	Friday	Saturday	Difference
Castleton	_____ °F	_____ °F	_____ °F
Newtown	_____ °F	_____ °F	_____ °F
Bellville	_____ °F	_____ °F	_____ °F
Discovery	_____ °F	_____ °F	_____ °F

Use the pattern block of each shape to draw two larger figures. One example has been done for you.

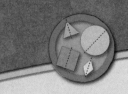

Create a Shape

Use the pattern block of each shape to draw two larger figures. One example has been done for you.

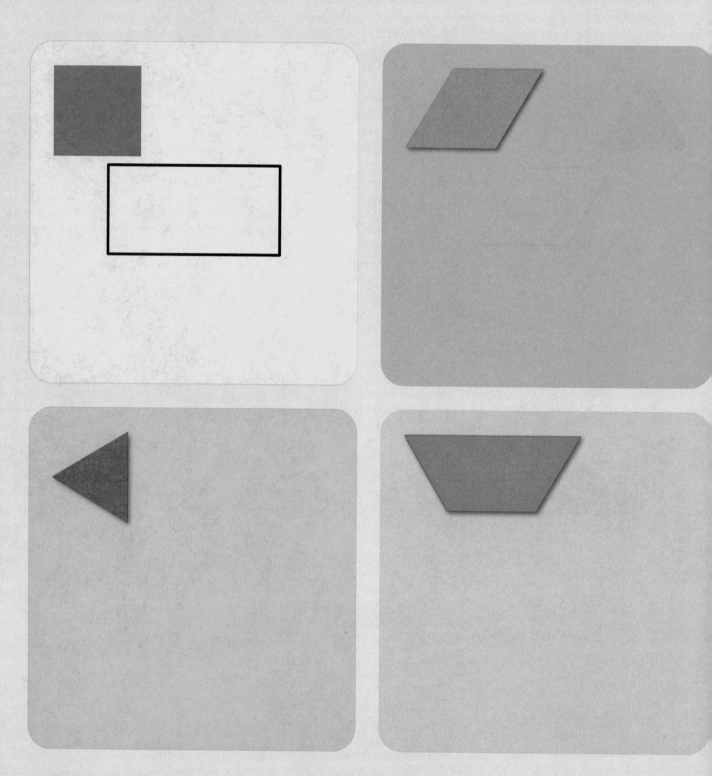

Look at each set of shapes. What attributes are the shapes sorted by? Draw blocks to create a new sort. Write the attributes for the new sort and draw the shapes.

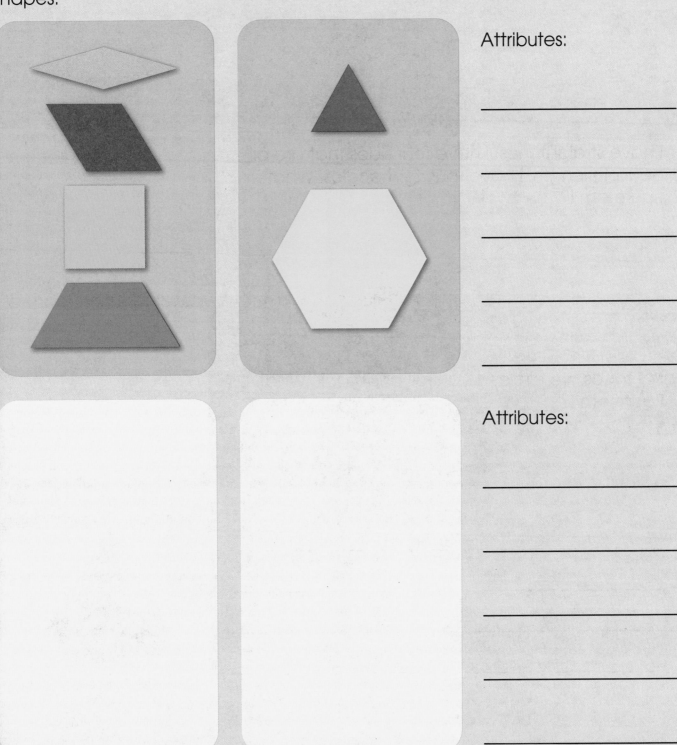

Attributes:

_____

_____

_____

_____

_____

Attributes:

_____

_____

_____

_____

_____

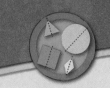

What Am I?

Solve each riddle. Draw and write the name of the two- or three-dimensional figure described. Write your own riddle for the last figure.

I have straight lines. I have four sides that are all equal in length. I have four right angles. What figure am I?

_____

My faces are circles. I can roll and stack. What figure am I?

_____

_____

_____

_____

_____

square pyramid

Name That Figure!

Circle the word that describes each object.

cube

cylinder

sphere

cone

cylinder

sphere

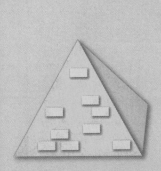

cone

sphere

pyramid

cube

cone

sphere

sphere

cone

rectangular prism

cube

cone

pyramid

The Great Shape Sort

Follow the directions.

1. Color each circle.
2. Outline each shape that has 4 sides.
3. Circle each small shape.
4. Draw an X on each square.
5. Draw a dot in each shape with 3 sides.

Read each description. Circle the correct figure. You may circle more than one figure in each row.

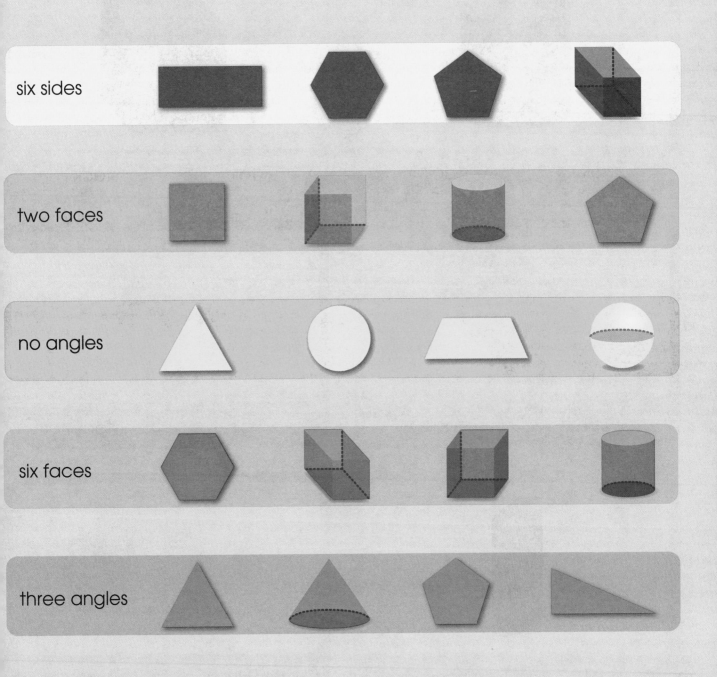

six sides

two faces

no angles

six faces

three angles

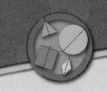

Stack and Roll

Look at each figure. Decide if it will roll, stack, or do both. Circle the answer(s).

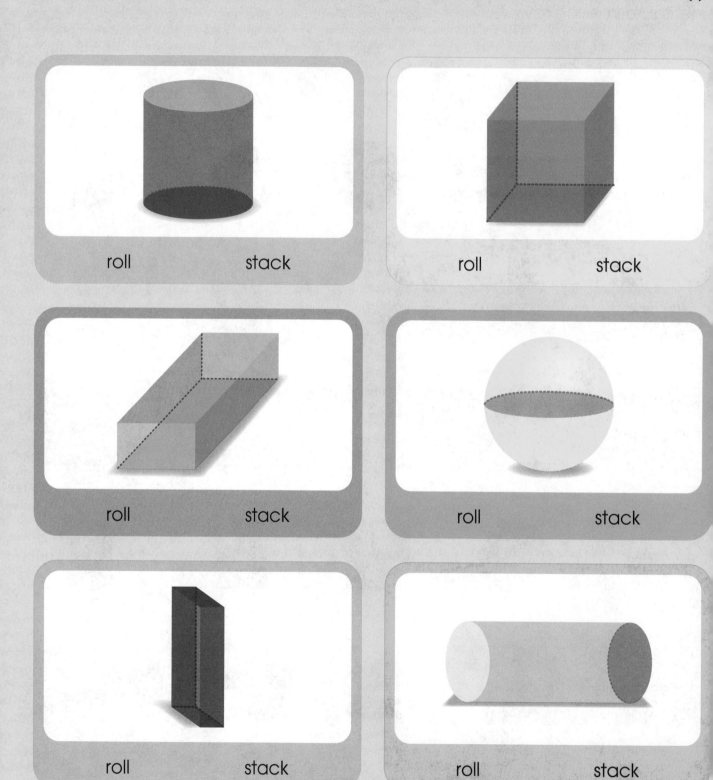

roll   stack

roll   stack

roll   stack

roll   stack

roll   stack

roll   stack

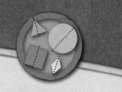

A tangram is a puzzle that has 7 pieces, or tans. Trace the tangram on a separate piece of paper. Cut the tangram you drew into 7 pieces. Match the tans to the shapes in the yellow square. Then, rearrange the tans in the blue box and trace them to make a new picture.

What can you make?

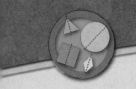

Tangrams

Use the tangram you made on the previous page to answer the questions.

Are any of the shapes congruent? Similar? What other shape can you make by putting together the 2 small triangles?

Draw a picture using 2 hexagons, 6 triangles, 1 trapezoid, 3 squares, and 2 rhombuses.

Look at the picture you drew on the previous page. Where is the trapezoid? What word(s) describe the trapezoid's position? Describe the picture you drew using position words such as above, beside, etc.

Penguin Path

Help the penguin get to the fish. On a separate sheet of paper, write the number of steps the penguin needs to take and the directions she needs to travel (north, south, east, or west).

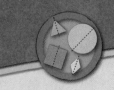

Penguin Path

Use your work from the previous page to answer the questions. How many steps did the penguin take in all? Did the penguin take more steps north or more steps south? If another penguin followed your directions, would it end up in the same place as this penguin?

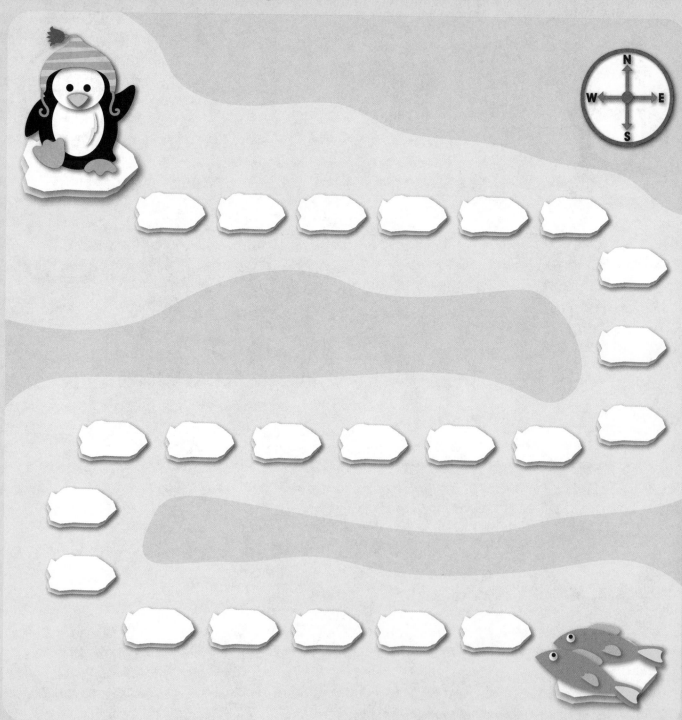

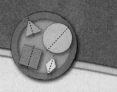

Use the zoo map to answer each question.

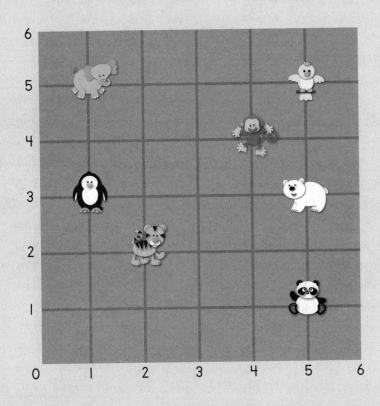

Which animal is near the tigers?

_____

Which animal is farthest
from the pandas?

_____

Which animal can be
found at (5,3)?

_____

Where are the birds located?

_____

Draw a **Z** at (3,6) to show where the
zoo entrance is located.

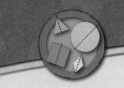

At the Zoo

Use the zoo map to answer each question.

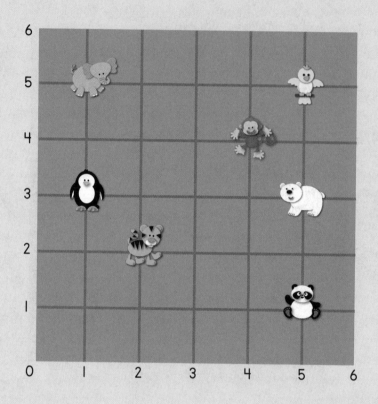

At what coordinates are the monkeys located?

_____

At what coordinates are the pandas located?

_____

Are the tigers and the birds near or far from each other? How do you know?

_____

How many squares down from the birds must you go to get to the polar bears?

_____

Draw how each letter would look after a slide, a flip, and a turn.

H

slide   flip   turn

P

slide   flip   turn

S

slide   flip   turn

T

slide   flip   turn

Congruent or Similar?

Look at each set of shapes. Write congruent, similar, or neither. Draw examples of congruent and similar shapes in the boxes.

congruent

similar

Look at the shapes and then answer the questions.

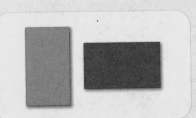

What does it mean if two shapes are congruent?

_____

What does it mean if two shapes are similar?

_____

_____

How can two shapes be neither similar nor congruent?

_____

Two circles are sometimes congruent and always similar. Two of what other shapes are sometimes congruent and always similar?

_____

Alphabet Symmetry

Circle each letter of the alphabet that has symmetry. Draw Xs on the letters that do not have symmetry.

A B C D E F
G H I J K L
M N O P Q R
S T U V W X
Y Z

Alphabet Symmetry

Look at the letters of the alphabet and answer the questions.

How many uppercase letters of the alphabet are symmetrical?

_____

Can a shape have more than one line of symmetry?

_____

What letter has the most lines of symmetry?

_____

Which uppercase letters are not symmetrical?

_____

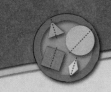

Complete the chart by drawing the correct face for each three-dimensional figure. Then, write the name of each shape that is a face.

figure		
	cylinder	cube
face		
	_____	_____

Complete the chart by drawing the correct face for each three-dimensional figure. Then, write the name of each shape that is a face.

figure		
	pyramid	cone
face		

Look at each outlined shape. Use the length of each side to write a number sentence. Then, use the number sentence to find the perimeter.

_____ + _____ + _____ + _____ + _____ = _____

P = _____

_____ + _____ + _____ + _____ = _____

P = _____

Find the Perimeter

Look at each outlined shape. Use the length of each side to write a number sentence. Then, use the number sentence to find the perimeter.

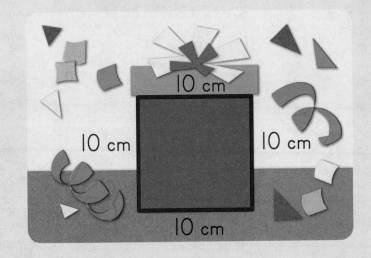

_____ + _____ + _____ + _____ = _____

P = _____

_____ + _____ + _____ = _____

P = _____

I Spy Shapes

Look around the room for objects that have shapes like those in the picture below. Find at least two objects that are each type of shape. Circle the shapes below when you find them.

Time Will Tell

Circle the unit of time you would use to measure each activity. Then, write the order of the units of time from 1 to 6, with 1 being the shortest unit of time.

brush your teeth

minutes   hours

_____

take a vacation

minutes   days

_____

build a house

minutes   days

hours   months

_____

grow a tree

years   days

_____

tie your shoes

seconds   minutes

_____

bake a cake

hours   weeks

_____

Time and Time Again

Read the times. Draw the hands and write the numbers for each time given.

five o'clock

three thirty

quarter after one

quarter to six

seven o'clock

five minutes after two

Draw the hands to show the time. Repeat for each clock.

The Hands of Time

Write the numbers to show the time. Repeat for each clock.

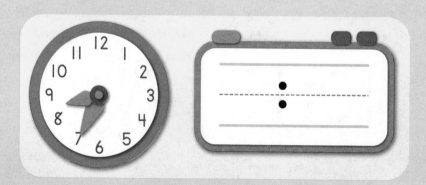

The Hands of Time

Draw the hands to show the time. Repeat for each clock.

1:10

7:55

4:25

2:40

The Hands of Time

Write the numbers to show the time. Repeat for each clock.

Time and Time Again

Read the times. Draw the hands and write the numbers for each time given.

quarter to five

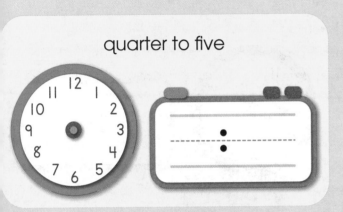

quarter after two

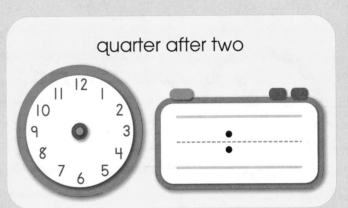

five minutes after one

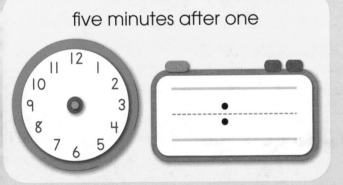

eight o'clock

four thirty

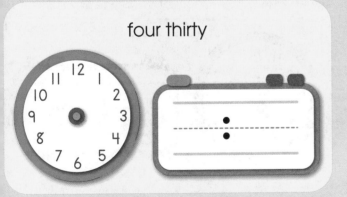

nine thirty

What Time Is It?

Look at each clock. Write the time.

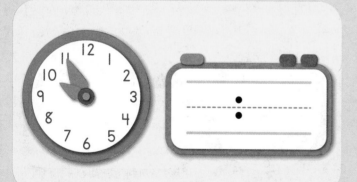

What Time Is It?

Look at each clock. Write the time.

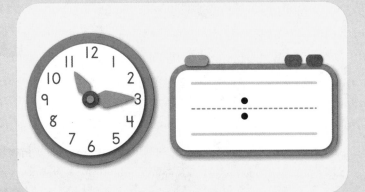

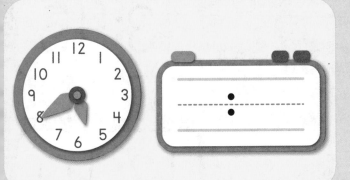

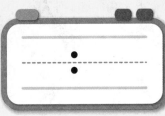

Discover Second Grade

129

© Carson-Dellosa
CD-704891

Match the time on the clock with the digital time.

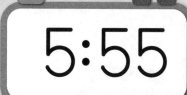

5:55

10:25

2:35

3:45

12:10

Match the time on the clock with the digital time.

6:20

7:30

1:40

4:15

11:05

Elapsed Laps

Read each word problem. Draw the hands on the first clock to show the start time for the swimmer's laps. Draw the hands on the last clock to show the end time for the laps.

Start

Katie arrived at swim practice at 3:30. She swam her warm-up laps in 30 minutes. What time did she finish?

End

Start

Brady arrived at swim practice at 4:00. He finished his warm-up laps in 45 minutes. What time did he finish?

End

Start

Ethan arrived at swim practice at 3:45. He finished his warm-up laps in 20 minutes. What time did he finish?

End

Elapsed Laps

Read each word problem. Draw the hands on the first clock to show the start time for the swimmer's laps. Draw the hands on the last clock to show the end time for the laps.

Start   **End**

Lisa arrived at swim practice at 2:30. She swam her warm-up laps in 30 minutes. What time did she finish?

Start   **End**

Tom arrived at swim practice at 3:00. He finished his warm-up laps in 35 minutes. What time did he finish?

Start   **End**

Jake arrived at swim practice at 2:45. He finished his warm-up laps in 40 minutes. What time did he finish?

A Balancing Act

Write the names of two objects or draw two objects on each scale to make the picture true.

A Balancing Act

Write the names of two objects or draw two objects on each scale to make the picture true.

Biggest Blankets

Use buttons to find the area (A) of each blanket.

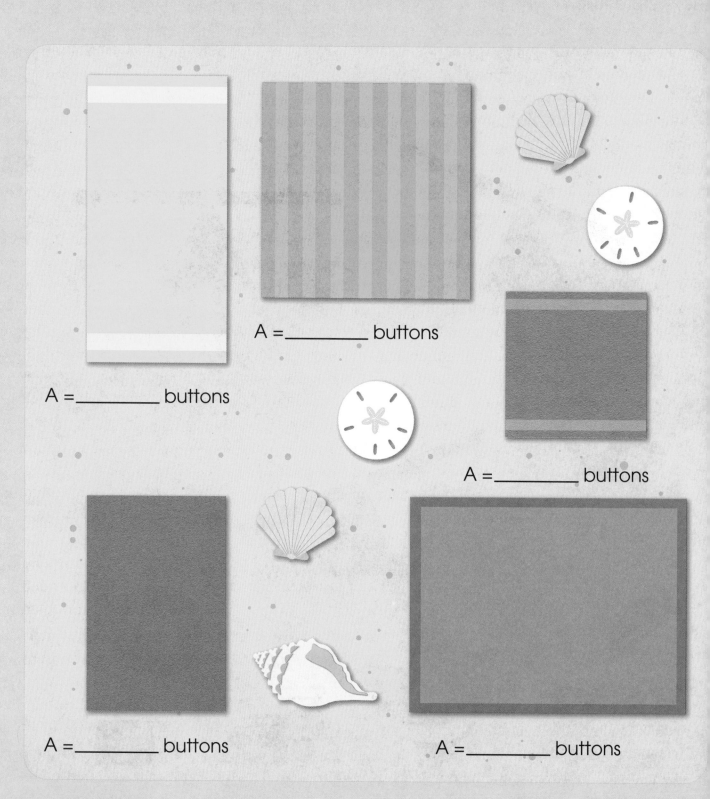

A =_____ buttons

A =_____ buttons

A =_____ buttons

A =_____ buttons

A =_____ buttons

Use buttons to find the area (A) of each letter.

A = _____ buttons

A = _____ buttons

Penny Counts

Measure the length of each object with pennies. Write the measurement on the line.

_____ penny

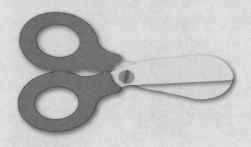

_____ pennies

_____ pennies

Measure the length of each object with pennies. Write the measurement on the line.

_____ pennies

_____ pennies

_____ pennies

Measure the length of each bug with paper clips. Write the measurement on the line.

The ladybug is about _____ paper clip(s) long.

The bee is about _____ paper clip(s) long.

Measure the length of the butterfly with paper clips. Write the measurement on the line.

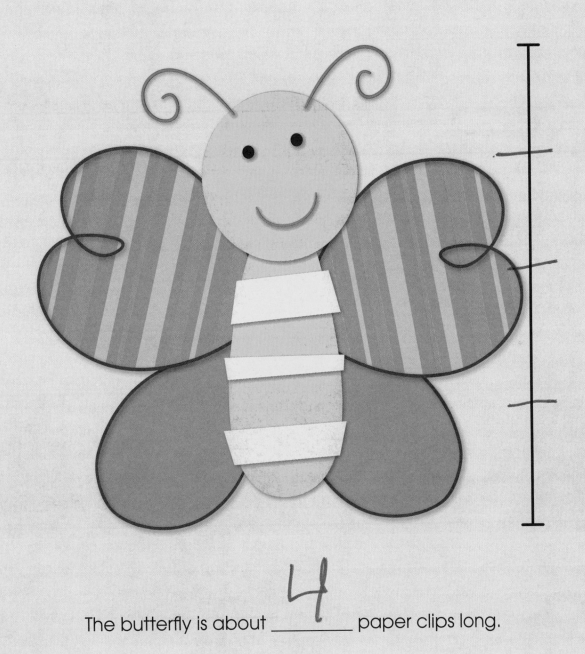

The butterfly is about __4__ paper clips long.

Measure Up!

Estimate the length of a desk or a table. Then, measure it with each item.

Estimate: _____ paper clips long

Actual: _____ paper clips long

Estimate: _____ pencils long

Actual: _____ pencils long

Estimate: _____ paintbrushes long

Actual: _____ paintbrushes long

Estimate: _____ scissors long

Actual: _____ scissors long

Ribbon Measurement

Use the width of your thumb to measure the length of each ribbon.

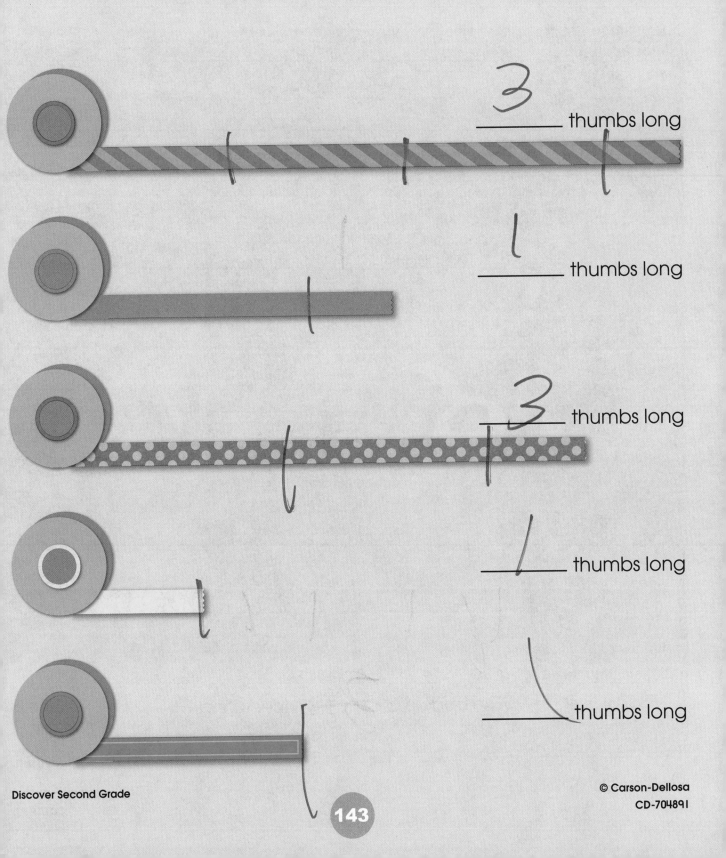

_3_ thumbs long

_l_ thumbs long

_3_ thumbs long

_l_ thumbs long

____ thumbs long

Darling Dogs

Measure each dog with a ruler.

The pug is _____1_____ inch long.

The beagle is _____3_____ inches long.

Measure each dog with a ruler.

The poodle is _____ 2 _____ inches long.

The dachshund is _____ 5 _____ inches long.

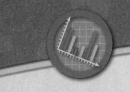

Sort a set of buttons by color. Complete the tally chart to show your data. Then, answer the questions.

Color	Number

How many total buttons are there? _____

Which color appears the most? _____

Which color appears the least? _____

Look at the shirts. How would you sort and classify them into groups? Label each side of the Venn diagram with an attribute. Then, write each shirt number in the correct section.

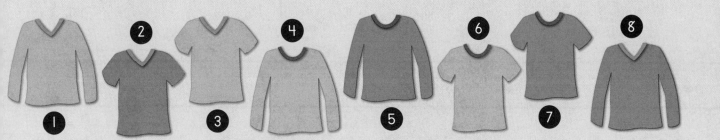

_____   both   _____

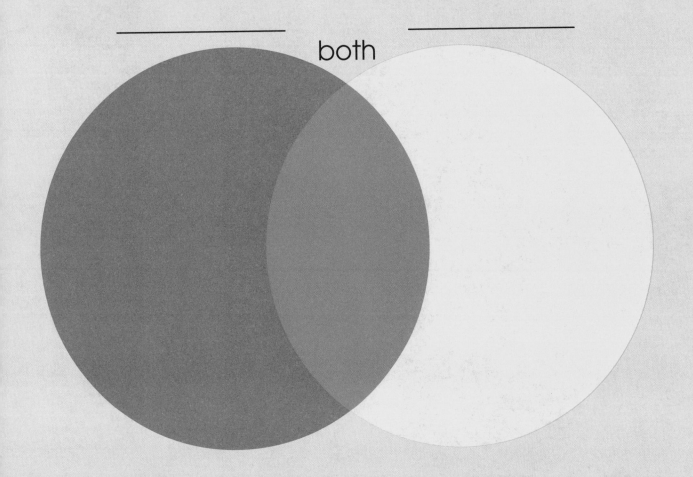

One for the Money

Sort a handful of coins. Arrange the pennies, nickels, dimes, and quarters on the graph to show how many of each coin you have.

 1¢

 5¢

 10¢

 25¢

Totals: _____ pennies, _____ nickels, _____ dimes, _____ quarters

Pennies and Nickels

Count the coins and write the amount.

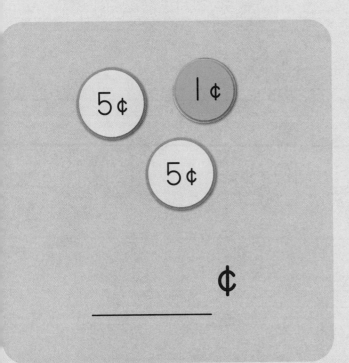

_____ ¢

_____ ¢

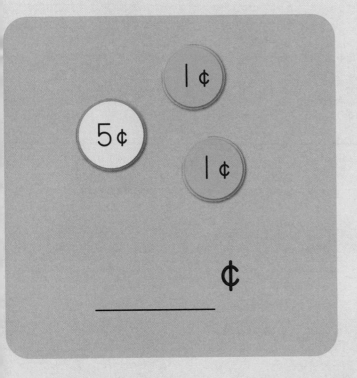

_____ ¢

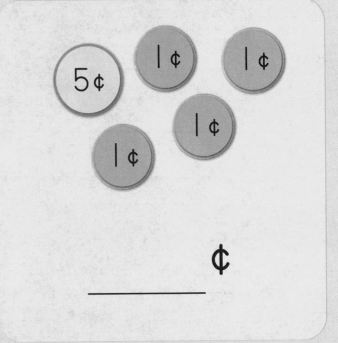

_____ ¢

Pennies, Nickles, and Dimes

Count the coins and write the amount.

10¢   5¢
1¢

_____ ¢

10¢   5¢
10¢   1¢
10¢   1¢
1¢

_____ ¢

10¢   5¢
5¢   5¢   1¢

_____ ¢

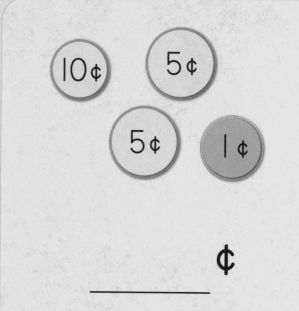

10¢   5¢
5¢   1¢

_____ ¢

Draw a line from the toy to the amount of money it costs.

36¢

68¢

43¢

57¢

22¢

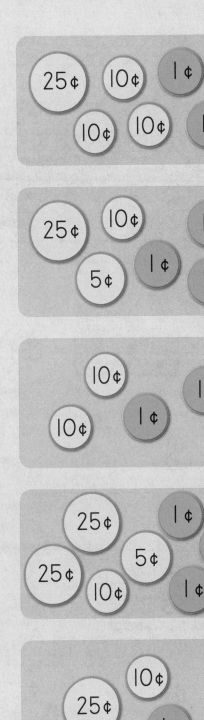

Counting Money

Count the money and write the amounts.

10¢ 10¢ 10¢ 10¢ 10¢
10¢ 10¢ 10¢ 10¢ 10¢

$ ____ . _____

25¢ 25¢
25¢ 25¢

$ ____ . _____

$1   25¢

$ ____ . _____

$1

10¢ 10¢ 1¢

$ ____ . _____

$1   25¢ 25¢
5¢

$ ____ . _____

25¢ 25¢ 10¢ 10¢ 1¢
25¢ 25¢   5¢   1¢

$ ____ . _____

Draw a line from each food item to the correct amount of money.

$1.59

$.77

$1.95

$1.27

$.89

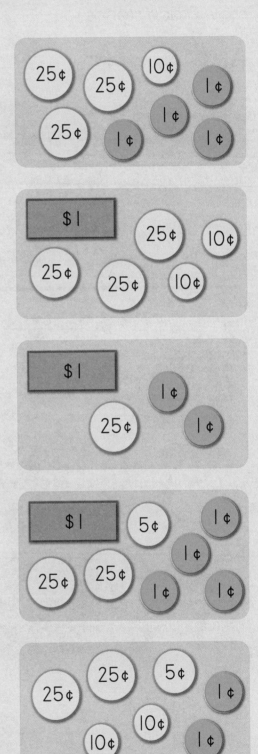

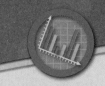

Preferred Pets

Look at the results of a class survey about favorite pets. Draw smiley faces to show the data in a pictograph. Look at the key to see how many votes each smiley face stands for.

卌 I

卌 卌 IIII

IIII

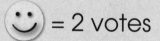 = 2 votes

Look at the results of a class survey about favorite foods. Draw smiley faces to show the data in a pictograph. Look at the key to see how many votes each smiley face stands for.

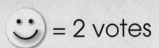 = 2 votes

© Carson-Dellosa

CD-704891

Ice Cream Flavors

Look at the bar graph to see how many scoops of each ice cream flavor a shop sold in one day. Record the data by making tally marks in the matching colored scoops.

Ice Cream Flavors

Look at the bar graph to see how many scoops of each ice cream flavor a shop sold in one day. Record the data by making tally marks in the matching colored scoops.

Ice Cream Sales for July 8

Maria graphed how her pet Fluffy spent each hour for one day. Use the information from the circle graph to write the number of hours Fluffy spent doing each activity.

How Fluffy Spent Her Day

Activity	Hours
Sleeping	
Eating	
Playing	
Digging	
Cuddling	
Scratching	

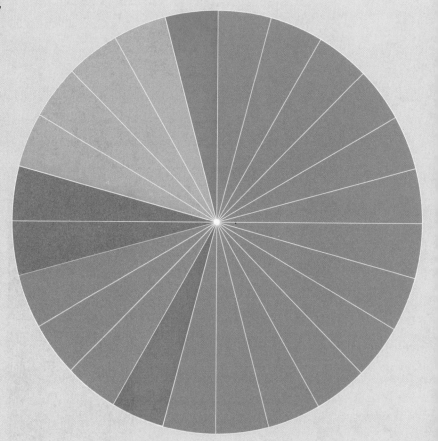

Angela graphed how her pet Spike spent each hour for one day. Use the information from the circle graph to write the number of hours Spike spent doing each activity.

How Spike Spent His Day

Activity	Hours
Sleeping	
Eating	
Playing	
Digging	
Cuddling	
Scratching	

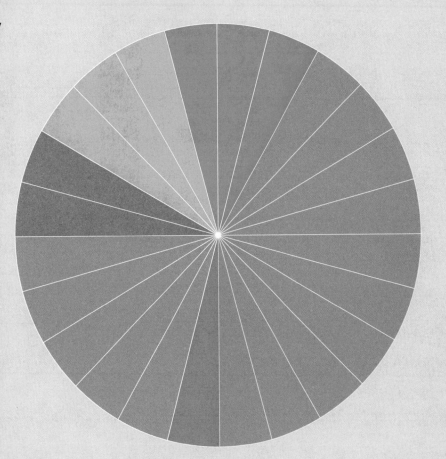

© Carson-Dellosa

CD-704891

Snow Day!

Use the graph of snowfall amounts to answer each question.

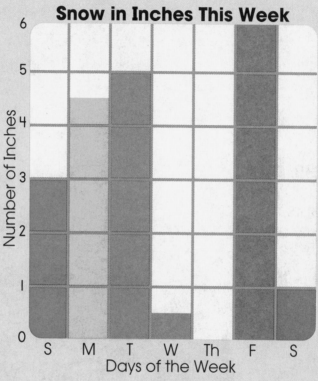

How many total inches of snow fell this week?

_____

Which two days together have a snowfall total of 8 inches?

_____

_____

How many more inches did it snow on Friday than on Monday?

_____

Write a true statement about the snowfall data based on the graph.

_____

_____

Use the graph of rainfall amounts to answer each question.

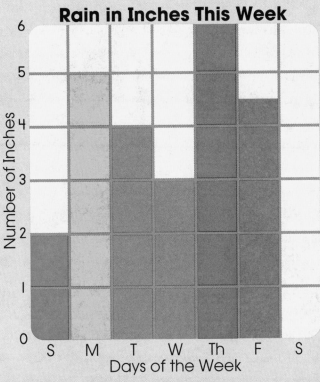

Rain in Inches This Week

Number of Inches

Days of the Week

How many total inches of rain fell this week?

_____

Which two days together have a rainfall total of 11 inches?

_____

_____

How many more inches did it rain on Monday than on Sunday?

_____

Write a true statement about the rainfall data based on the graph.

_____

_____

Could You?

Think about the probability of each statement. Circle likely, more likely, or less likely after each statement.

With one penny:

You will flip heads.

likely   **more likely**   **less likely**

You will flip tails.

likely   **more likely**   **less likely**

You will flip the coin on its edge.

likely   **more likely**   **less likely**

hink about the probability of each statement. Circle more likely or less likely
after each statement.

With two dice:

You will roll a 6.

more likely   **less likely**

You will roll a 12.

more likely   **less likely**

You will roll a 7.

more likely   **less likely**

Fair Game

Use a paper clip and a pencil to make a pointer for the spinners below. Spin each spinner 20 times. Write the winner's name for each spin in the correct chart.

Spin	Winner
1	
2	
3	
4	
5	
6	
7	
8	
9	
10	
11	
12	
13	
14	
15	
16	
17	
18	
19	
20	

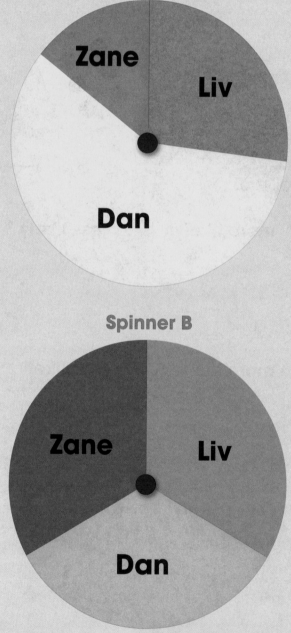

Spinner A

Zane

Liv

Dan

Spinner B

Zane

Liv

Dan

Spin	Winner
1	
2	
3	
4	
5	
6	
7	
8	
9	
10	
11	
12	
13	
14	
15	
16	
17	
18	
19	
20	

Answer the questions based on the spinners shown below.

What makes a spinner fair? Which spinner is fair?

_____

Spinner A

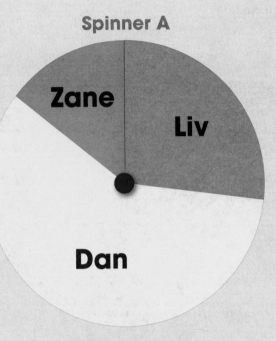

What color is the first spinner most likely to land on? Why?

_____

Is it likely that Zane will win with Spinner A? Why or why not?

_____

What color are you most likely to land on with Spinner B?

_____

Spinner B

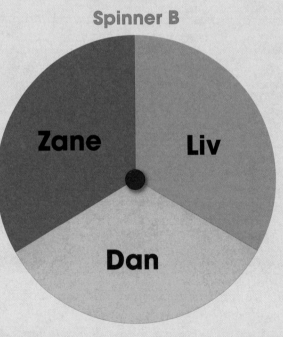

Is it likely that Liv will win with Spinner B? Why or why not?

_____

_____

_____

Color 2 pieces of paper red, 5 blue, and 1 yellow. Put them in a bag.

Close your eyes and pull a piece of paper out of the bag. Open your eyes and look at the piece of paper. Make a tally mark in the correct column to show which color you pulled. Repeat this 10 times.

Language Arts

All About Me!

Fill in the blanks to tell all about you!

Name _____
(First)   (Last)

Address _____

City _____

State _____

Phone number _____

Age _____

Places I have visited: _____

_____

_____

_____

My favorite vacation: _____

_____

_____

_____

Fill in the beginning consonant for each word. Then, color the pictures.

Example: ____c____ at

_____ ag

_____ ish

_____ oat

_____ orse

_____ og

_____ ellyfish

Fill in the beginning consonant for each word. Then, color the pictures.

Example: __r__ ibbon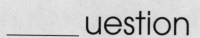

____ arker

____ uestion

____ adybug

____ aper clip

____ ids

____ otebook

Fill in the beginning consonant for each word. Then, color the pictures.

Example: __s__ cissors

____ebra

____urtle

____-ray

____est

____o-yo

____orm

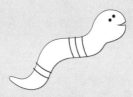

Fill in the ending consonant for each word. Then, draw and color a picture of something else that ends with **b**, **d**, **f**, or **g**.

pyrami____

scar____

ladybu____

bir____

cra____

Fill in the ending consonant for each word. Then, draw and color a picture of something else that ends with **k**, **l**, **m**, **n**, **p**, or **r**.

balloo ____

ar ____

dinne ____

des ____

paper cli ____

cerea ____

Ending Consonants: s, t, x

Fill in the ending consonant for each word. Then, draw and color a picture of something else that ends with **s**, **t**, or **x**.

elephan____

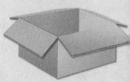

bo ____

bu ____

hear____

ne ____

Consonant blends are two or three consonant letters in a word whose sounds combine, or blend. **Examples: br, fr, gr, pr, tr**

Look at each picture. Say its name. Write the blend you hear at the beginning of each word. Then, color the pictures.

_____   _____   _____

_____   _____   _____

_____   _____   _____

Blends: br, fl, pl, sk, sn

Look at the pictures and say their names. Write the letters for the beginning sound in each word.

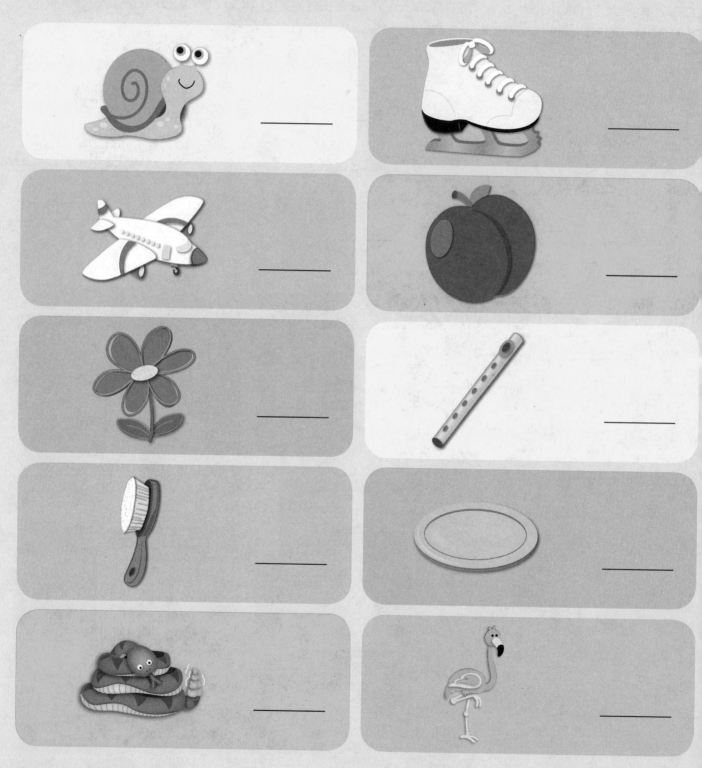

Blends: bl, cl, cr, sl

Look at the pictures and say their names. Write the letters for the beginning sound in each word. Then, color the pictures.

_____ayon

_____anket

_____acker

_____ock

_____ock

_____oud

_____ed

_____ab

_____am

Consonant Blends

Write a word from the word box to answer each riddle.

| clock | glass | blow | climb | slipper |
| sleep | gloves | clap | blocks | flashlight |

You need me when the lights go out.
What am I?

_____

People use me to tell the time.
What am I?

_____

You put me on your hands in the winter
to keep them warm. What am I?

_____

Cinderella lost one like me at midnight.
What am I?

_____

This is what you do with your hands when
you are pleased. What is it?

_____

You can do this with a whistle or with
bubble gum. What is it?

_____

These are what you might use to build a castle
when you are playing. What are they?

_____

You do this to get to the top of a hill.
What is it?

_____

This is what you use to drink water.
What is it?

_____

You do this at night with your eyes closed.
What is it?

_____

Consonant Blends

Consonant blends can be made up of three letters whose sounds combine.

Examples: **spl** and **scr**

Read the words in the box. Write a word from the word box to finish each sentence. Circle the consonant blend in each word. **Hint:** There are three letters in each blend.

splash screw	screen sprain	spray split	street strong	scream string

Did you _____ your ankle?

I tied a _____ to my tooth to help pull it out.

I have many friends who live on my _____.

We always _____ when we ride the roller coaster.

A _____ helps keep bugs out of the house.

It is fun to _____ in the water.

My father uses an ax to _____ the firewood.

We will need a _____ to fix the chair.

You must be very _____ to lift this heavy box.

The firemen _____ the fire with water.

© Carson-Dellosa
CD-704891

Consonant Teams: sh, ch, wh, th

Consonant teams are two or three consonant letters that have a single sound. **Examples: sh** and **tch**

Look at the first picture in each row. Circle the pictures that have the same sound.

wheel

wh

shoe

sh

chicken

ch

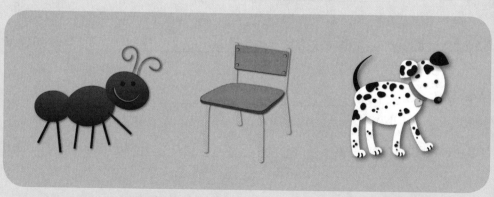

Consonant Teams

Circle the consonant teams in each word. Use the word box. Write a word from the word box to finish each sentence. Circle the consonant teams in your words. Remember: Consonant teams form one single sound. They are different from blends.

trash	ship	chair	which	catch
shut	splash	when	chain	patch

My _____ does not rock.

I put a _____ on my bike so nobody can take it.

We watched the big _____ dock and let off its passengers.

It is my job to take out the _____.

I have to wear a _____ over my eye until it is better.

The baby likes to _____ in the bathtub.

Can you _____ the ball with one hand?

Please _____ the windows before it rains.

_____ are we going to leave for school?

I don't know _____ of these books is mine.

Consonant Blends and Teams

Look at the words in the word box. Write all of the words that end with the **ng** sound in the column under the picture of the **ring**. Write all of the words that end with **nk** sound under the picture of the **junk**. Then, finish the sentences with words from the word box.

| strong | rank | bring | bank | honk | hang | thank |
| long | hunk | song | stung | bunk | sang | junk |

ring **ng**

junk **nk**

_____

_____

_____

_____

_____

_____

_____

_____

_____

_____

_____

_____

_____ your horn when you get to my house.

He was _____ by a bee.

We are going to put our money in a _____.

I want to _____ you for the birthday present.

My brother and I sleep in _____ beds.

Silent Letters

Some words have letters you can't hear at all, such as the **gh** in **night**, the **w** in **wrong**, the **l** in **walk**, the **k** in **knee**, the **b** in **climb**, and the **t** in **listen**.

Look at the words in the word box. Write the word under its picture. Underline the silent letters. Then, draw and color pictures for the other words.

knife	light	calf	wrench	lamb	eight
night	whistle	comb	thumb	knob	knee

_____   _____   _____

_____   _____

Hard and Soft c

When **c** is followed by **e**, **i**, or **y**, it usually has a **soft** sound. The **soft c** sounds like **s**. For example, **c**ircle and fen**c**e. When **c** is followed by **a**, **o**, or **u**, it usually has a **hard** sound. The **hard c** sounds like **k**.

Example: **c**up and **c**art

Read the words in the word box. Write the words in the correct lists. One word will be in both. Write a word from the word box to finish each sentence.

pencil dance	popcorn candy	tractor cookie	cent circus	mice card

Words with soft c

pencil

_____

_____

_____

_____

Words with hard c

_____

_____

_____

_____

_____

Another word for a penny is a _____.

A cat likes to chase _____.

You will see animals and clowns at the _____.

Will you please sharpen my _____?

When **g** is followed by **e**, **i**, or **y**, it usually has a **soft** sound. The **soft g** sounds like **j**.

Example: chan**g**e and **g**entle   When **g** is followed by **a**, **o**, or **u**, it usually has a hard sound, like the **g** in **g**o or **g**ate.

Look at the **c** and **g** words at the bottom of the page. Cut them out and glue them in the correct box below.

Soft sounds

Hard sounds

jug	gem	giant	crayon
grass	goat	grow	age
juice	face	engine	cart

This page is blank for the cutting activity on the opposite side.

Hard g and Soft g

Read the words in the word box. Write the words in the correct lists. Then, write a word from the box to finish each sentence.

engine giant	glove flag	cage large	magic glass	frog goose

Words with soft g

engine

_____

_____

_____

_____

Words with hard g

_____

_____

_____

_____

_____

Our bird lives in a _____.

Pulling a rabbit from a hat is a good _____ trick.

A car needs an _____ to run.

A _____ is a huge person.

An elephant is a very _____ animal.

Short Vowels

Vowels can make **short** or **long** sounds. The short **a** sounds like the **a** in c**a**t. The short **e** is like the **e** in l**e**g. The short **i** sounds like the **i** in p**i**g. The short **o** sounds like the **o** in b**o**x. The short **u** sounds like the **u** in c**u**p.

Look at each picture. Write the missing short vowel.

____ctopus

s ____n

k ____ds

c ____t

____lephant

d ____g

sk ____nk

____mbrella

p ____n

Cut out the giant vowels. Decorate them with pictures or words that have the short vowel sound.

This page is blank for the cutting activity on the opposite side.

This page is blank for the cutting activity on the opposite side.

CD-704891

Long Vowels

Long vowels have the same sounds as their names. When a **Super Silent e** comes at the end of a word, you can't hear it, but it changes the short vowel sound to a long vowel sound.

For example: rope, skate, cute, line

Say the name of the pictures. Listen for the long vowel sounds. Write the missing long vowel sound under each picture. Then, draw and color another picture that has a long vowel sound.

c ___ ke

pl ___ ne

n ___ se

gr ___ pe

k ___ te

R-Controlled Vowels

When a vowel is followed by the letter **r**, it has a different sound.

For example: **he** and **her**

Write a word from the word box to finish each sentence. Notice the sound of the vowel followed by an **r**.

| park | chair | horse | bark | bird |
| hurt | girl | hair | store | ears |

A dog likes to _____.

You buy food at a _____.

Children like to play at the _____.

An animal you can ride is a _____.

You hear with your _____.

A robin is a kind of _____.

If you fall down, you might get _____.

The opposite of a boy is a _____.

You comb and brush your _____.

You sit down on a _____.

R-Controlled Words

R-controlled vowel words are words in which the **r** that comes after the vowel changes the sound of the vowel.

For example: bird, star, burn

Write the correct word in the sentences below.

horse	jar	dirt	purple	bird	turtle

Jelly comes in one of these. _____

This creature has feathers and can fly. _____

This animal lives in a shell. _____

This animal can pull wagons. _____

If you mix water and this, you will have mud. _____

This color starts with the letter **p**. _____

Answer the riddles below. You will need to complete the words with the correct vowel followed by **r**.

I am something you may use to eat. What am I?

f _____ k

My name means the opposite of tall. What am I?

sh _____ t

I can be seen high in the sky. I twinkle. What am I?

st _____

I am a kind of clothing a girl might wear. What am I?

sk _____ t

I am the word for a group of cows. What am I?

h _____ d

I am a part of your body. What am I?

_____ m

Double Vowel Sounds

Usually when two vowels appear together, the first one says its name and the second one is silent.

Example: **b<u>e</u>an**

Unscramble the double vowel words below. Write the correct word on the line. Then, draw and color something else that has a double vowel sound, such as seat, tear, goat, or peas.

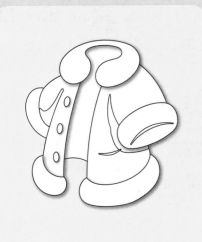

ocat _____

atil _____

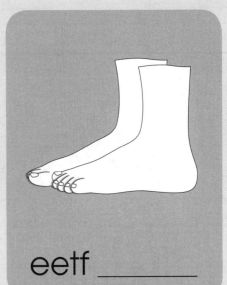

eetf _____

otab _____

apil _____

Vowel Teams

The vowel teams **ou** and **ow** can have the same sound. You can hear it in the words **clown** and **cloud**. The vowel teams **au** and **aw** have the same sound. You hear it in the words **cause** and **law**.

Look at the pictures. Write the correct vowel team to complete each word. The first one is done for you. You may need to use a dictionary to help you with the correct spelling. In the last box, draw and color a picture of a word with a vowel team. Some examples: owl, paw, saw, and clown

__au__ to

h ___ se

fl ___ er

m ___ th

m ___ se

The vowel team **ea** can have a short **e** sound like in **head** or a long **e** like in **bead**. An **ea** followed by an **r** makes a sound like the one in **ear** or the one in **heard**.

Read the story. Listen for the sound ea makes in the bold words.

Have you ever **read** a book or **heard** a story about a **bear**? You might have **learned** that bears sleep through the winter. Some bears may sleep the whole season. Sometimes they look almost **dead**! But they are very much alive. As the cold winter passes and the spring **weather** comes **near**, they wake up. After such a nice rest, they must be **ready** to **eat** a **really** big **meal**!

Words with long ea	Words with short ea	ea followed r
_____	_____	_____
_____	_____	_____
_____	_____	_____
_____	_____	_____

The vowel team **ie** makes the long **e** sound as in **believe**. The team **ei** also makes the long **e** sound as in **either**. But **ei** can also make a long **a** sound as in **vein**. The teams **eigh** and **ey** also make the long a sound.

Circle the words with the long **a** sound.

neighbor	veil
receive	reindeer
reign	ceiling

Finish the sentences with words from the word box. Some words have the long **a** sound, and some have the long **e** sound.

chief	sleigh	obey	weigh	thief	field	ceiling

Eight reindeer pull Santa's _____.

Rules are for us to _____.

The bird got out of its cage and flew up to the _____.

The leader of an Indian tribe is the _____.

How much do you _____?

They caught the _____ who took my bike.

Corn grows in a _____.

Look at the first picture in each row. Color the pictures that have the same sound. For the last row, draw and color something that has the same **oi** sound (Examples: coin, boil).

toy **oy**

mouse **ou**

brown **ow**

foil **oi**

Vowel Teams: ai, ee

Write the vowel team **ai** or **ee** to complete each word. Then, draw something that has the vowel team **ai** or **ee**.

r__ __n

n __ __ l

b __ __

wh __ __ l

m __ __ l

Y as a Vowel

When **y** comes at the end of a word, it is a vowel. When **y** is the only vowel at the end of a one-syllable word, it has the sound of long **i** (as in **my**). When **y** is the only vowel at the end of a word with more than one syllable, it has the sound of long **e** (as in **baby**).

Look at the words in the word box. If the word has the sound of long **i**, write it under the word **my**. If the word has the sound of long e, write it under the word **baby**. Then, write the word from the word box that answers each riddle.

| happy | penny | fry | try | sleepy | dry |
| bunny | why | windy | sky | party | fly |

my

_____

_____

_____

_____

_____

baby

_____

_____

_____

_____

It takes five of these to make a nickel. _____

This is what you call a baby rabbit. _____

It is often blue, and you can see it if you look up. _____

You might have one of these on your birthday. _____

It is the opposite of wet. _____

You might use this word to ask a question. _____

Y as a Vowel

Read the rhyming story. Choose the words from the box to fill in the blanks.

| Larry | money | honey | Mary | funny | bunny |

_____ and _____ are friends.

Larry is selling _____. Mary needs _____

to buy the honey. "I want to feed it to my _____," said Mary.

Larry laughed and said, "That is _____. Everyone knows that

bunnies do not eat honey."

Y as a Vowel

Read the story. Choose the words from the box to fill in the blanks.

try	my	Why	cry	shy	fly

Sam is very _____. Ann asks, "Would you like to

_____ my kite?" Sam starts to _____.

Ann asks, "_____ are you crying?"

Sam says, "I'm afraid to _____."

"Oh, _____! You are a good kite flyer!" cries Ann.

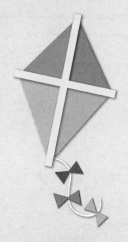

Fill in the blanks with a word from the word box. Then, draw a picture to show one of the sentences.

| pencil | recess | fun | teacher | math | crayons |

I need to sharpen my _____.

School is _____!

My _____ helps me learn.

I need to color the picture with _____.

I play kickball at _____.

In _____, I can add and subtract.

Days of the Week

Write the day of the week that answers each question. Then, draw a picture to show your favorite day of the week.

Sunday Monday	Tuesday Wednesday	Thursday Friday	Saturday

What is the first day of the week? _____

What is the last day of the week? _____

What day comes after Tuesday? _____

What day comes between Wednesday and Friday? _____

What is the third day of the week? _____

What day comes before Saturday? _____

What day comes after Sunday? _____

© Carson-Dellosa
CD-704891

Compound Words

Compound words are two words that are put together to make one new word.

Mix words from the first column with words from the second column to make new words. Write your new words on the lines at the bottom of the page.

grand

snow

fish

down

rose

shoe

note

moon

bowl

light

stairs

string

book

mother

ball

bud

_____   _____

_____   _____

_____   _____

_____   _____

Cut out the words below. Glue them together in the box to make compound words.

Can you think of any more compound words?

Compound Words

sun	air	mail	ball
box	room	water	guard
foot	living	class	flower
plane	room	melon	body

This page is blank for the cutting activity on the opposite side.

Compound Words

Read the sentences. Fill in each blank with a compound word from the box.

| raincoat | doghouse | mailbox | sunglasses | flowerpot |

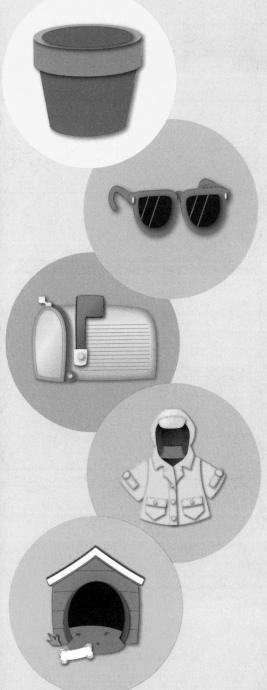

A pot for flowers is a _____.

Glasses for sun are _____.

A box for mail is a _____.

A coat for the rain is a _____.

A house for a dog is a _____.

Compound Words

Draw a line under the compound word in each sentence. On the line, write two words that make up each compound word. Then, draw a picture for each compound word.

A <u>firetruck</u> came to help put out the fire.

_____

I will be nine years old on my next birthday.

_____

We built a treehouse in the yard.

_____

Dad put a scarecrow in the garden.

_____

It is fun to make footprints in the snow.

_____

I like to read the comics in the newspaper.

_____

Cowboys ride horses and use lassos.

_____

Contractions are a short way to write two words.

Examples: **it is = it's**   **is not = isn't**   **I have = I've**

Cut out and glue each of the contractions next to the correct word pair.

Contractions

I am

it is

you are

we are

they are

she is

he is

she's	they're	we're	he's
I'm	it's	you're	

This page is blank for the cutting activity on the opposite side.

Cut out the two words and put them together to show which two words make the contraction. Then, glue them over the contraction.

This page is blank for the cutting activity on the opposite side.

Contractions

Circle the contraction that would replace the underlined words. Write the contraction. Then, draw and color a picture to show each sentence.

Example: **were not = weren't**

The boy _____ sad.
      wasn't   weren't

We _____ working.
  wasn't   weren't

Jen and Caleb _____ eaten lunch yet.
        haven't   hasn't

The mouse _____ been here.
      haven't   hasn't

Syllables

Words are made up of parts called **syllables**. Each syllable has a vowel sound. One way to count the syllables is to clap as you say the word.

Examples:
cat   1 clap   1 syllable
table   2 claps   2 syllables
butterfly   3 claps   3 syllables

"Clap out" the words below. Write how many syllables each word has.

movie _____   dog _____

piano _____   basket _____

tree _____   swimmer _____

bicycle _____   rainbow _____

sun _____   paper _____

cabinet _____   picture _____

football _____   run _____

television _____   enter _____

Syllables

Dividing a word into syllables can help you read a new word. You also might divide syllables when you are writing if you run out of space on a line.

Many words contain two consonants that are next to each other. A word can usually be divided between the consonants.

Divide each word into two syllables. The first one is done for you.

kitten   <u>kit ten</u>

harder   _____

lumber   _____

dirty   _____

batter   _____

sister   _____

winter   _____

little   _____

funny   _____

dinner   _____

Syllables

One way to help read a word you don't know is to divide it into parts called **syllables**. Every syllable has a vowel sound.

Say the words. Write the number of syllables. Then, draw a picture of one of the words. The first one has been done for you.

bird _____1_____

rabbit _____

apple _____

elephant _____

balloon _____

family _____

candy _____

butterfly _____

popcorn _____

puddle _____

yellow _____

Syllables

When a double consonant is used in the middle of a word, the word can usually be divided between the consonants.

Look at the words in the word box. Divide each word into two syllables. Leave space between each syllable. One is done for you.

butter	puppy	kitten	yellow
dinner	chatter	ladder	happy
pillow	letter	mitten	summer

but ter _____ _____

_____ _____ _____

_____ _____ _____

_____ _____ _____

Many words are divided between two consonants that are not alike.

Look at the words in the word box. Divide each word into two syllables. One is done for you.

window	doctor	number	carpet
mister	winter	pencil	candle
barber	sister	picture	under

win dow _____ _____

_____ _____ _____

_____ _____ _____

© Carson-Dellosa
CD-704891

Syllables

Write the number 1 or 2 on the line to tell how many syllables are in each word. If the word has 2 syllables, draw a line between the syllables. Then, draw a picture of one of the words.

Example: sup|per

dog _____

timber _____

bedroom _____

cat _____

slipper _____

street _____

tree _____

chalk _____

batter _____

blanket _____

Haiku

A **haiku** is a Japanese form of poetry.

first line: 5 syllables
second line: 7 syllables
third line: 5 syllables

Example:

The squirrel is brown.
He lives in a great big tree.
He eats nuts all day.

Write your own haiku. Draw a picture to go with it.

A **suffix** is a letter or group of letters that is added to the end of a word to change its meaning.

Add the suffixes to the root words to make new words. Use your new words to complete the sentences.

help + ful = _____

care + less = _____

build + er = _____

talk + ed = _____

love + ly = _____

loud + er = _____

My mother _____ to my teacher about my homework.

The radio was _____ than the television.

Sally is always _____ to her mother.

A _____ put a new garage on our house.

The flowers are _____.

It is _____ to cross the street without looking both ways.

An **ing** at the end of an action word shows that the action is happening now. An **ed** at the end shows the action happened in the past.

Look at the words in the word box. Underline the root word in each one. Write a word to complete each sentence.

snowing talking	wished played	eating looking	doing

We like to play. We _____ yesterday.

Is that snow? Yes, it is _____.

Did you wish for a new bike? Yes, I _____ for one.

Who is doing the dishes? I am _____ them.

Did you talk to your friend? Yes, we are _____ now.

Will you look at my book? I am _____ at it now.

I like to eat pizza. We are _____ it for lunch.

Suffixes

Read the story. Underline the words that end with **est**, **ed**, or **ing**. On the lines below, write the root word for each word you underlined.

The funniest book I ever read was about a girl named Nan. Nan did everything backward. She even spelled her name backward. Nan slept during the day and played at night. She dried her hair before washing it. She turned on the light after she finished her book, which she read from the back to the front! When it rained, Nan waited until she was inside before opening her umbrella. She even walked backward. The silliest part: The only thing Nan did forward was back up!

_____   _____   _____

_____   _____   _____

_____   _____   _____

_____   _____

_____

Cut out the root words at the bottom of the page and glue them next to the correct word.

coming

rained

lived

carried

visited

sitting

hurried

swimming

running

racing

run	live	hurry	swim
visit	carry	come	race
	rain	sit	

This page is blank for the cutting activity on the opposite side.

A **prefix** is a letter or group of letters that is added to the beginning of a word to change its meaning. The prefix **re** means "again."

Read the story. Then, follow the instructions.

> Kim wants to find ways she can save the Earth. She studies the "three Rs" —reduce, reuse, and recycle. *Reduce* means "to make less." Both *reuse* and *recycle* mean "to use again."

Add **re** to the beginning of each word below. Use the new words to complete the sentences.

_____ build

_____ fill

_____ read

_____ tell

_____ write

_____ run

The race was a tie, so Dawn and Kathy had to _____ it.

The block wall fell down, so Simon had to _____ it.

The water bottle was empty, so Luna had to _____ it.

Javier wrote a good story, but he wanted to _____ it to make it better.

The teacher told a story, and students had to _____ it.

Toni didn't understand the directions, so she had to _____ them.

Read the story. Change **Unlucky Sam** to **Lucky Sam** by removing the **un** prefix from the **bold** words. Write the new words in the new story. Then, draw a picture of Lucky Sam.

Unlucky Sam

Sam was **unhappy** about a lot of things in his life. His parents were **uncaring**. His teacher was **unfair**. His big sister was **unkind**. His neighbors were **unfriendly**. He was **unhealthy**, too! How could one boy be as **unlucky** as Sam?

Lucky Sam

Sam was _____ about a lot of things in his life.

His parents were _____. His teacher was

_____. His big sister was _____. His neighbors

were _____. He was _____ , too! How could

one boy be as _____ as Sam?

Prefixes

Read the story. Change the story by removing the prefix **re** from the **bold** words. Write the new words in the new story.

Repete is a **rewriter** who has to **redo** every story. He has to **rethink** up the ideas. He has to **rewrite** the sentences. He has to **redraw** the pictures. He even has to **retype** the pages. Who will **repay Repete** for all the work he **redoes**?

_____ is a _____ who has to

_____ every story. He has to _____ up

the ideas. He has to _____ the sentences. He has to

_____ the pictures. He even has to _____

the pages. Who will _____ _____ for all the

work he _____?

Discover Second Grade

231

© Carson-Dellosa
CD-704891

Read each sentence. Look at the words in **bold**. Circle the prefix and write the root word on line. Then, draw a picture to show one of the sentences.

The **preview** of the movie was funny.

_____

Please try to keep the cat **inside** the house.

_____

We will have to **reschedule** the trip.

_____

Are you tired of **reruns** on television?

_____

I have **outgrown** my new shoes already.

_____

You just have **misplaced** the papers.

_____

Police **enforce** the laws of the city.

_____

I **disliked** that book.

_____

Try to **enjoy** yourself at the party.

_____

Parts of a Book

A book has many parts. The **title** is the name of the book. The **author** is the person who wrote the words. The **illustrator** is the person who drew the pictures. The **table of contents** is located at the beginning to list what is in the book. The **glossary** is a little dictionary in the back to help you with unfamiliar words. Books are often divided into smaller sections of information called **chapters**.

Look at one of your books. Answer the questions about your book.

The title of my book is _____ .

The author is _____ .

The illustrator is _____ .

My book has a table of contents.   Yes or No

My book has a glossary.   Yes or No

My book is divided into chapters.   Yes or No

Recalling Details: Nikki's Pets

Read about Nikki's pets. Then, answer the questions.

Nikki has two cats, Tiger and Sniffer, and two dogs, Fluffy and Wiggles. Tiger is an orange cat who likes to sleep under a big tree and pretend she is a real tiger. Sniffer is a gray cat who likes to sniff the flowers in Nikki's garden. Fluffy is a gray poodle with fluffy white tufts of fur. Wiggles is a big, furry brown dog who wiggles all over when he is happy.

Which dog is brown and furry? _____

What color is Tiger? _____

What kind of dog is Fluffy? _____

Which cat likes to sniff flowers? _____

Where does Tiger like to sleep? _____

Who wiggles all over when he is happy? _____

Read the story about baby animals. Then, answer the questions.

Baby cats are called kittens. They love to play. A baby dog is a puppy. Puppies chew on old shoes. They run and bark. A lamb is a baby sheep. Lambs eat grass. A baby duck is called a duckling. Ducklings swim with their wide, webbed feet. Foals are baby horses. A foal can walk the day it is born! A baby goat is a kid. Some people call children kids, too!

A baby cat is called a _____ .

A baby dog is a _____ .

A _____ is a baby sheep.

_____ swim with their webbed feet.

A _____ can walk the day it is born.

A baby goat is a _____ .

Read about the yo-yo trick.

Wind up the yo-yo string. Hold the yo-yo in your hand. Now, hold your palm up. Throw the yo-yo downward on the string. Hold your palm down. Now, swing the yo-yo forward. Make it "walk." This yo-yo trick is called "walk the dog."

Number the directions in order.

_____ Swing the yo-yo forward and make it "walk."

_____ Hold your palm up and drop the yo-yo.

_____ Turn your palm down as the yo-yo reaches the ground.

Sequencing

Cut out the pictures and glue them in the correct order.

This page is blank for the cutting activity on the opposite side.

Sequencing: Baking a Cake

Read about baking a cake. Then, write the missing steps.

Dylan, Dana, and Dad are baking a cake. Dad turns on the oven. Dana opens the cake mix. Dylan adds the eggs. Dad pours in the water. Dana stirs the batter. Dylan pours the batter into the cake pan. Dad puts it in the oven.

1. Turn on the oven.

2. _____

3. Add the eggs.

4. _____

5. Stir the batter.

6. _____

7. _____

Sequencing: Making a Card

Read about how to make a card. Then, follow the instructions.

You will need scissors, glue, and colored paper. First, look at all your old cards. Then, cut out what you like. Now, fold the colored paper in half. Glue the cut-outs to the front of your card. Write your name inside.

Write the steps in order for making a card.

1.   Look at all your old cards.

2.   _____

3.   _____

4.   _____

Write your name inside.

On a separate sheet of paper, draw a picture of a new card you could make.

Same/Different: Stuffed Animals

Kate and Olivia like to collect and trade stuffed animals.

Draw two stuffed animals that are alike and two that are different.

Alike

Different

Same/Different: Cats and Tigers

Read about cats and tigers. Then, complete the Venn diagram, telling how they are the same and different.

Tigers are a kind of cat. Pet cats and tigers both have fur. Pet cats are small and tame. Tigers are large and wild.

Pet Cats   **Both**   **Tigers**

Read about Marvin and Mugsy. Then, complete the Venn diagram, telling how they are the same and different.

Marcy has two dogs, Marvin and Mugsy. Marvin is a black and white spotted Dalmatian. Marvin likes to run after balls in the backyard. His favorite food is Canine Crunchy Crunch. Marcy likes to take Marvin for walks because dogs need exercise. Marvin loves to sleep in his doghouse. Mugsy is a big, furry brown and white dog who wiggles when she is happy. Since she is big, she needs lots of exercise. So Marcy takes her for walks in the park. Her favorite food is Canine Crunchy Crunch. Mugsy likes to sleep on Marcy's bed.

Marvin   **Both**   **Mugsy**

A **simile** is a figure of speech that compares two different things. The words **like** or **as** are used in similes.

Draw a line to the picture that goes with each set of words.

as happy as a

as hungry as a

as quiet as a

as quick as a

as easy as

as cold as

as tiny as an

Classifying

Living things need air, food, and water to live. **Non-living** things are not alive.

Cut out the words at the bottom of the page. Glue each word in the correct column.

Living	Non-living

flower	book	boy	dog
chair	bread	tree	camera
car	horse	ant	shoe

This page is blank for the cutting activity on the opposite side.

Classifying

Read the sentences. Write the words from the word box where they belong.

bush airplane Stop	rocket wind truck	cake candy Poison	thunder rain flower	bicycle car pie	Danger grass bird

These things taste sweet.

_____   _____   _____

These things come when it storms.

_____   _____   _____

These things have wheels.

_____   _____   _____

These are words you see on signs.

_____   _____   _____

These things can fly.

_____   _____   _____

These things grow in the ground.

_____   _____   _____

Classifying: Animal Habitats

Read the story. Then, write each animal's name under **Water** or **Land** to tell where it lives.

Animals live in different habitats. A *habitat* is the place of an animal's natural home. Many animals live on land and others live in water. Most animals that live in water breathe with gills. Animals that live on land breathe with lungs.

fish	shrimp	giraffe	dog
cat	eel	whale	horse
bear	deer	shark	jellyfish

Water

_____   _____

_____   _____

_____   _____

Land

_____   _____

_____   _____

_____   _____

Comprehension: Playful Cats

read about cats. Then, follow the instructions.

Cats make good pets. They like to play. They like to jump. They like to run. Do you?

Cats make good _____ .

Write three things cats like to do.

_____

_____

_____

Think of a good name for a cat.
Write it on the line and then
draw a picture of a cat.

_____

Read about playing store. Then, answer the questions and draw a picture to show the main idea.

> Tyson and his friends like to play store. They use boxes and cans. They line them up. Then, they put them in bags.

Circle the main idea.

Tyson and his friends use boxes, cans, and bags to play store.

You need bags to play store.

Who likes to play store? Circle your answer.

all kids   some kids

Do you like to play store? _____

Read about paper bag puppets. Then, follow the instructions.

It is easy to make a hand puppet. You need a small paper bag. You need colored paper. You need glue. You need scissors. Are you ready?

Circle the main idea.

You need scissors.

Making a hand puppet is easy.

Write the four objects you need to make a paper bag puppet.

_____

_____

_____

_____

Draw a face on the paper bag puppet.

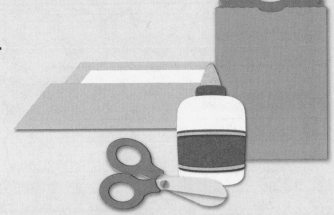

Read about winter. Then, follow the instructions.

It is cold in winter. Most kids like to play outdoors. Some kids make a snowman. Some kids skate. What do you do in winter?

Circle the main idea.

Snow falls in winter.

In winter, there are many things to do outside.

Write two things about winter weather.

_____

_____

Write what you like to do in winter. Then, draw a picture.

_____

_____

_____

_____

Read about the color of fish. Then, follow the instructions.

All fish live in water. Fish that live at the top are blue, green, or black. Fish that live down deep are silver or red. The colors make it hard to see the fish.

List the colors of fish at the top.

_____   _____   _____

List the two colors of fish that live down deep.

_____   _____

Color the top fish and the bottom fish the correct colors.

Predicting Outcomes

Complete the story. Then, draw pictures to match the four parts.

Sylvia and Marge are flying a kite.

Beginning

_____
_____

Middle

The kite gets stuck in a tree.

Middle

_____
_____

End

Predicting Outcomes

Draw pictures to create your own story in the squares. Show the beginning, middle, and end in the appropriate boxes.

Beginning (Setting)

Middle (Problem)

Middle (Problem)

End (Solution)

Fact and Opinion: Henrietta the Humpback

Read the story. Then, follow the instructions.

My name is Henrietta, and I am a humpback whale. I live in cold seas in the summer and warm seas in the winter. My long flippers are used to move forward and backward. I like to eat fish. Sometimes, I show off by leaping out of the water. Would you like to be a humpback whale?

Write **F** next to each fact and **O** next to each opinion.

_____ Being a humpback whale is fun.

_____ Humpback whales live in cold seas during the summer.

_____ Whales are fun to watch.

_____ Humpback whales use their flippers to move forward and backward

_____ Henrietta is a great name for a whale.

_____ Leaping out of the water would be hard.

_____ Humpback whales like to eat fish.

_____ Humpback whales show off by leaping out of the water.

Read about Ryan's globe. Then, follow the instructions.

Ryan got a new globe. He wanted to place it where it would be safe. He asked his dad to put it up high. Where can his dad put the globe?

Write where Ryan's dad can put the globe.

_____

_____

Draw a place Ryan's dad can put the globe.

Making Inferences: Visualizing

Read the story about Melinda. Then, draw pictures that describe each part of the story.

Beginning: It was Halloween. Melinda's costume was a black cat with super-duper-polka-dot sunglasses.

Middle: Her little brown dog, Marco, yelped and ran under a big red chair when he saw her come into the room.

End: Melinda took off her black cat mask and sunglasses. Then, she held out a dog biscuit. She picked Marco up and hugged him. Then, he was happy.

Juniper has three problems to solve. She needs your help.
Read each problem. Write what you think she should do.

Juniper is watching her favorite TV show when the power goes out.

_____

_____

_____

Juniper is riding her bike to school when the front tire goes flat.

_____

_____

_____

Juniper loses her father while shopping in the supermarket.

_____

_____

_____

Draw three pictures to tell a story about each topic.

Feeding a pet

Beginning

Middle

End

Playing with a friend

Beginning

Middle

End

Six children from the same neighborhood travel to school in a different way. Can you find out how each one gets to school?

Read the clues. Draw a dot to show how each child travels to school. Draw **X**s on the remaining boxes.

	Brian	Gina	Lawrence	Luna	Taylor	Marianna
car						
bus						
walk						
bicycle						
truck						
van						

Clues:

Lawrence likes to walk to school.

Taylor hates to walk, so his mother takes him in a car.

Luna lives next door to Lawrence and waves to Gina as Gina goes by in a pickup truck.

Brian joins his friends on the bus.

Gina's friend, who lives next door to Lawrence, rides a bike to school.

Marianna likes to sit on the middle bench while riding to school.

Fiction is a make-believe story. **Non-fiction** is a true story.
Read about tornadoes. Then, follow the instructions.

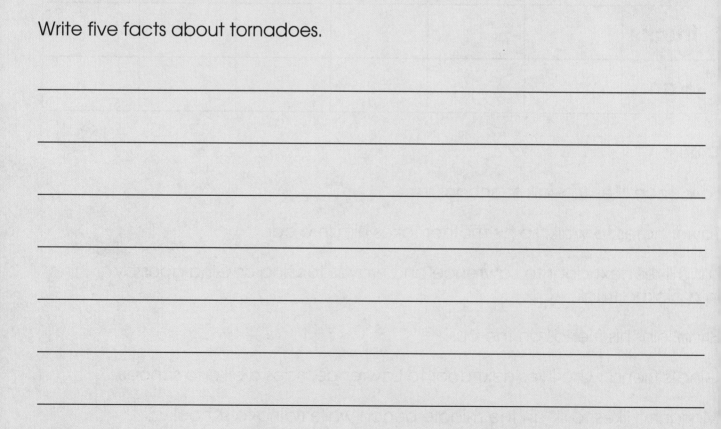

A tornado begins over land with strong winds
and thunderstorms. The spinning air becomes a
funnel. It can cause damage. If you are inside, go
to the lowest floor of the building. A basement is
a safe place. A bathroom or closet in the middle
of a building can be a safe place, too. If you are outside, lie in a ditch.
Remember, tornadoes are dangerous.

Write five facts about tornadoes.

_____

_____

_____

_____

_____

_____

The setting is where a story takes place. The characters are the people in a story or play.

Read about Hercules and answer the questions. Then, draw a picture to show a part of the story.

Hercules was born in the warm Atlantic Ocean. He was a very small and weak baby. He wanted to be the strongest hurricane in the world. But he had one problem. He couldn't blow 75-mile-per-hour winds. Hercules blew and blew in the ocean, until his sister Hola told him it would be more fun to be a breeze than a hurricane. Hercules agreed. It was a breeze to be a breeze!

What is the setting of the story? _____

Who are the characters? _____

What is the problem? _____

_____

How does Hercules solve his problem?

_____

_____

_____

Read each story. Then, write whether it is fiction or nonfiction.

One sunny day in July, a dog named Stan ran away from home. He went up one street and down the other looking for fun, but all the yards were empty. Where was everybody? Stan kept walking until he heard the sound of band music and happy people. Stan walked faster until he got to Central Street. There he saw men, women, children, and dogs getting ready to walk in a parade. It was the Fourth of July!

Fiction or Nonfiction? _____

Americans celebrate the Fourth of July every year because it is the birthday of the United States of America. On July 4, 1776, the United States got its independence from Great Britain. Today, Americans celebrate this holiday with parades, picnics, and fireworks as they proudly wave the red, white, and blue American flag.

Fiction or Nonfiction? _____

Read about fiction and nonfiction books. Then, follow the instructions.

There are many kinds of books. Some books have make-believe stories about princesses and dragons. Some books contain poetry and rhymes, like Mother Goose. These are fiction.

Some books contain facts about space and plants. And still other books have stories about famous people in history like Abraham Lincoln.

Write **F** for fiction and **NF** for nonfiction.

_____ nursery rhyme

_____ fairy tale

_____ true life story of a famous athlete

_____ Aesop's fables

_____ dictionary entry about foxes

_____ weather report

_____ story about a talking tree

_____ story about how a tadpole becomes a frog

_____ story about animal habitats

_____ riddles and jokes

Write a story telling what you like to do. Then, draw a picture to go with your story on another sheet of paper.

_____

_____

_____

_____

_____

_____

_____

_____

_____

_____

ABC Order

Put the words in ABC order on the bags.

grapes

bread

soup

apples

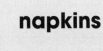

napkins

rolls

ice cream

pizza

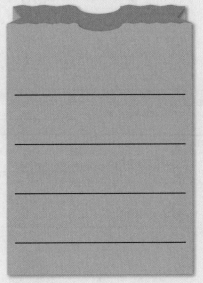

carrots

bananas

treats

potatoes

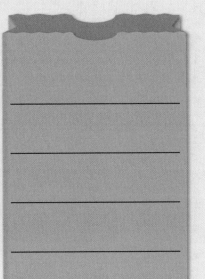

rice

soda

cups

beans

ABC Order

Write these words in order. If two words start with the same letter, look at the second letter in each word.

Example: **lamb**
               light
               Lamb comes first because **a** comes before **i** in the alphabet.

tree   _____

branch   _____

leaf   _____

rain   _____

umbrella _____

cloud   _____

dish   _____

dog   _____

bone   _____

mail   _____

stamp   _____

slot   _____

ABC Order

verb
noun

Cut out the scoops of ice cream at the bottom of the page. Place them on the correct cone in alphabetical order.

lemon

dog

truck

frost

apple

house

ring

This page is blank for the cutting activity on the opposite side.

Synonyms

Words that mean the same or nearly the same thing are called **synonyms**. Read each sentence. Fill in the blanks with the synonyms.

| friend | tired | story | presents | little |

I want to go bed because I am very <u>sleepy</u>. _____

On my birthday, I like to open my <u>gifts</u>. _____

My <u>pal</u> and I like to play together. _____

My favorite <u>tale</u> is *Cinderella*. _____

The mouse was so <u>tiny</u> that it was hard to catch him. _____

Antonyms are words that mean the opposite of another word.

Examples:

hot and **cold**
short and **tall**

Draw a line from each word on the left to its antonym on the right.

sad	**white**
bottom	**stop**
black	**fat**
tall	**top**
thin	**hard**
little	**found**
cold	**short**
lost	**hot**
go	**big**
soft	**happy**

Antonyms: Words and Pictures

Anna and Luke often like to do opposite things. Help them design their new white shirts using opposites.

Think of a pair of antonyms. Write one on each shirt. Draw pictures on the shirts to match the antonyms.

Homophones

Homophones are words that sound alike but are spelled differently and have different meanings. Sometimes, homophones can be more than two words.

Examples:

Pear and **pair** are homophones.
To, **too**, and **two** are homophones.

Draw a line from each word on the left to its homophone on the right.

blue	knight
night	too
beet	blew
write	see
hi	meet
two	son
meat	bee
sea	high
be	right
sun	beat

Homophones: Birthday Cake

Read the sentences. The bold words are homophones. Then, follow the directions for a birthday cake.

The baker **read** a recipe to bake a cake. Color the plate he put it on **red**.

Draw a **hole** in the middle of the cake. Then, color the **whole** cake yellow.

Look **for** the top of the cake. Draw **four** candles there.

Write a sentence using the words **hole** and **whole**.

_____

Write a sentence using the words **read** and **red**.

_____

A **noun** is the name of a person, place, or thing.

Look through a magazine. Cut out pictures of nouns and glue them below. Write the name of the noun next to each picture.

Proper Nouns

Proper nouns are the names of specific people, places, and things. Proper nouns begin with a capital letter.

Write the proper nouns on the lines below. Use capital letters at the beginning of each word. Then, draw a picture of a place and label it. Make sure to use a capital letter.

mike smith

_____

lynn cramer

_____

tyler

_____

phantom

_____

raleigh, north carolina

_____

The days of the week and the months of the year are always capitalized.

Circle the words that are written correctly. On the line below, write the words that need capital letters.

sunday	July	Wednesday		
friday	tuesday	june	may	december
january	February	March	august	Monday
September	saturday	October	Thursday	April

Days of the Week

_____

_____

_____

_____

Months of the Year

_____

_____

_____

_____

Capitalization

The first word and all of the important words in a title begin with a capital letter.

Write the book titles on the lines below. Use capital letters.

dinosaurs

lizards everywhere

the magic cat

all about presidents

the space dog

gerbil care

_____

_____

_____

_____

_____

_____

Plurals are words that mean more than one. To make a word plural, you add an **s** or **es**. In some words ending in **y**, the **y** changes to an **i** before **es**. For example, **baby** changes to **babies**.

Look at the following lists of plural words. Next to each, write the word that means one. Then, draw a picture to show one of the words.

dresses _____

pencils _____

bushes _____

candies _____

foxes _____

wishes _____

chairs _____

boxes _____

shoes _____

ladies _____

stories _____

bunnies _____

puppies _____

desks _____

Pronouns

Pronouns are words that can be used instead of nouns. **She**, **he**, **it**, and **they** are pronouns.

Read the sentence. Then, write the sentence again, using **she**, **he**, **it**, or **they** in the blank. Draw a picture to show one of the sentences.

Dan likes funny jokes. _____ likes funny jokes.

Peg and Sam went to the zoo. _____ went to the zoo.

My mom's car was covered in snow. _____ was covered in snow.

Sara is a very good dancer. _____ is a very good dancer.

Fred and Ted are twins. _____ are twins.

The **subject** of a sentence is the person, place, or thing the sentence is about.

Underline the subject in each sentence. Then, draw pictures to show the sentences.

Example: <u>Mom</u> read a book.

(Think: Who is the sentence about? <u>Mom</u>)

The bird flew away.

The kite was high in the air.

The children played a game.

The books fell down.

The monkey climbed a tree.

Compound Subjects

Two similar sentences can be joined into one sentence if the predicate is the same. A **compound subject** is made up of two subjects joined together by a conjunction like **and**.

Example:

Jamie can sing.
Sandy can sing.
<u>Jamie **and** Sandy</u> can sing.

Combine the sentences. Write the new sentence on the line.

The cats are my pets.
The dogs are my pets.

_____

Chairs are in the store.
Tables are in the store.

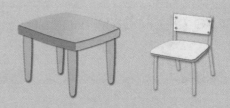

_____

Jen is wearing a red dress.
Alice is wearing a red dress.

_____

Verbs

A **verb** is the action word in a sentence. Verbs tell what something does or that something exists.

Example:

Run, **sleep**, and **jump** are verbs.

Circle the verbs in the sentences below. Then, draw a picture to show one of the sentences.

We play baseball every day.

Susan pitches the ball very well.

Mike swings the bat harder than anyone.

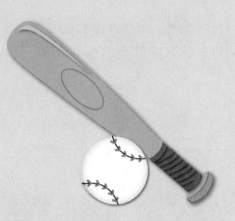

Chris slides into home base.

Laura hit a home run.

Verbs

We use verbs to tell when something happens. Sometimes, we add an **ed** to verbs that tell us if something has already happened.

Example:

Today, we will **play**. Yesterday, we **played**.

Write the correct verb in the blank. Then, draw a picture to show one of the sentences.

Today, I will _____ my dog, Fritz.
            wash   washed

Last week, Fritz _____ when we said, "Bath time, Fritz!"
            cry   cried

My sister likes to _____ wash Fritz.
            help   helped

One time she _____ Fritz by herself.
            clean   cleaned

Fritz will _____ a lot better after his bath.
            look   looked

Predicates

The **predicate** is the part of the sentence that tells about the action.

Circle the predicate in each sentence. Then, draw a picture to show one of the sentences.

Example: The boys (ran) on the playground.

Think: The boys did what?

The woman painted a picture.

The puppy chases his ball.

The students went to school.

Butterflies fly in the air.

The baby wants a drink.

Compound Predicates

A **compound predicate** is made by joining two sentences that have the same subject. The predicates are usually joined together by the word **and**.

Example:

Tom can jump.
Tom can run.
Tom can <u>run</u> **and** <u>jump</u>.

Combine the sentences. Write the new sentence on the line.

The dog can roll over.
The dog can bark.

_____

Sam is drawing.
Sam is coloring.

_____

Tara is tall
Tara is smart.

_____

The **subject** of the sentence is the person, place, or thing the sentence is about. The **predicate** is the part of the sentence that describes the subject or tells what the subject does.

Draw a line between the subject and the predicate. Underline the noun in the subject and circle the verb in the predicate. Then, draw a picture of one of the sentences.

Example: The furry <u>cat</u> | (ate) the food.

Mandy walks to school.

The bus drove the children.

The school bell rang very loudly.

The teacher spoke to the students.

The girls opened their books.

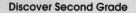

Compound Subjects and Predicates

The following sentences have either a compound subject or a compound predicate.

If the sentence has a compound subject (more than one thing doing the action), **underline** the subject. If it has a compound predicate (more than one action), **circle** the predicate.

Examples:

Bats and owls like the night.

The fox slinks and spies.

Ducks swim and quack.

Sloths climb and sleep in trees.

Bees and mosquitos fly.

Snakes slither and hiss.

Frogs and penguins swim.

Adjectives

Adjectives are words tell more about a person, place, or thing.

Examples: Cold, dark, fuzzy

Circle the adjectives in the sentences. Then, draw a picture to show one of the sentences.

The juicy apple is on the plate.

The furry dog is eating a bone.

It was a sunny day.

The cute kitten jumps on the couch.

The sky was dark.

Articles

 verb noun

Articles are small words that help us to better understand nouns. **A** and **an** are articles. We use **an** before a word that begins with a vowel. We use **a** before a word that begins with a consonant.

Example: We looked in **a** nest. It had **an** eagle in it.

Read the sentences. Write **a** or **an** in the blank.

I found _____ book.

It had a story about _____ ant in it.

In the story, _____ lion gave three wishes to _____ ant.

The ant's first wish was to ride _____ zebra.

The second wish was to ride _____ horse.

The last wish was _____ wish for three more wishes.

A **sentence** tells a complete idea. It has a noun and a verb. It begins with a capital letter and has punctuation at the end.

Circle the group of words if it is a sentence. Then, draw a picture to show one of the sentences.

Grass is a green plant.

Mowing the lawn.

Grass grows in fields and lawns.

Sheep, cows, and horses eat grass.

We like to play in.

A picnic on the grass.

Plant flowers around.

Statements

Statements are sentences that tell us something. They begin with a capital letter and end with a period.

Write the statements on the lines below. Begin each sentence with a capital letter and end it with a period. Then, draw a picture to show one of the sentences.

we like to ride our bikes

_____

we go down the hill very fast

_____

we keep our bikes shiny and clean

_____

we know how to change the tires

_____

Surprising sentences tell a strong feeling and end with an exclamation point. A surprising sentence may be only one or two words showing fear, surprise, or pain.

Example: Oh, no!

Put a period at the end of the sentences that tell something. Put an exclamation point at the end of the sentences that tell a strong feeling. Put a question mark at the of the sentences that ask a question.

The shark can swim very fast ☐

Wow ☐

Look at that shark go ☐

Can you swim fast ☐

Oh, my ☐

You're faster than I am ☐

Let's swim together ☐

We can swim as fast as a shark ☐

What fun ☐

Do you think sharks get tired ☐

Commands

Commands tell someone to do something.

Example: Be careful.

It can also be written as "Be careful!" if it tells a strong feeling.

Put a period at the end of the command sentences. Use an exclamation point if the sentence tells a strong feeling. Write your own commands on the lines below.

Clean your room ☐

Now ☐

Be careful with your goldfish ☐

Watch out ☐

Be a little more careful ☐

_____

_____

_____

_____

_____

_____

Questions are sentences that ask something. They begin with a capital letter and end with a question mark.

Write the questions on the lines below. Begin each sentence with a capital letter and end it with a question mark.

will you be my friend

_____

what is your name

_____

are you eight years old

_____

do you like rainbows

_____

We add **'s** to nouns (people, places, or things) to tell who or what owns something.

Read the sentences. Fill in the blanks to show ownership.

Example: The doll belongs to **Sara**.

It's **Sara's** doll.

Amy has a red bathing suit.

_____ bathing suit is red.

Jimmy has a white shirt.

_____ shirt is white.

The tail of the cat is short.

The _____ tail is short.

The name of my sister is Lisa.

My _____ name is Lisa.

Is, **are**, and **am** are special action words that tell us something is happening now.

Use **am** with I   Example: **I am.**

Use **is** to tell about one person or thing.   Example: **He is.**

Use **are** to tell about more than one.   Example: **We are.**

Use **are** with you.   Example: **You are.**

Write **is**, **are**, or **am** in the sentences below.

My friends _____ helping me build a tree house.

It _____ in my backyard.

We _____ using hammers, wood, and nails.

It _____ a very hard job.

I _____ lucky to have good friends.

Was and Were

Was and **were** tell us about something that already happened.

Use **was** to tell about one person or thing.

Example: **I was, he was**.

Use **were** to tell about more than one person or thing when using the words you.

Example: **We were, you were**.

Write **was** or **were** in each sentence.

Lily _____ eight years old on her birthday.

Tim and Steve _____ happy to be at the party.

Megan _____ too shy to sing "Happy Birthday."

Ben _____ sorry he dropped his cake.

All of the children _____ happy to be invited.

Go, Going, and Went

We use **go** or **going** to tell about now or later. Sometimes, we use **going** with the words **am** or **are**. We use **went** to tell about something that already happened.

Write **go**, **going**, or **went** in the sentences below. Then, color the pictures.

Today, I will _____ to the bakery.

Yesterday, Sally _____ to school.

I am _____ to take Lola to the vet.

Jan and Steve _____ to the party.

We are _____ to the beach.

Have, Has, and Had

We use **have** and **has** to tell about now. We use **had** to tell about something that already happened.

Write **has**, **have**, or **had** in the sentences below.

We _____ three cats at home.

Chet _____ orange fur.

Jack and Charlie _____ brown fur.

My friend Tom _____ one cat, but he ran away.

Tom _____ a new cat now.

See, Sees, and Saw

We use **see** or **sees** to tell about now. We use **saw** to tell about something that already happened.

Write **see**, **sees**, or **saw** in the sentences below.

Last night, we _____ the stars.

Joe can _____ the stars from his window.

He _____ them every night.

Last week, he _____ the Big Dipper.

Can you _____ it in the night sky, too?

If you _____ it, you would remember it.

Joe _____ it often now.

How often do you _____ it?

Eat, Eats, and Ate

We use **eat** or **eats** to tell about now. We use **ate** to tell about what already happened.

Write **eat**, **eats**, or **ate** in the sentences below. Then, draw a picture of one of your favorite foods to eat.

We like to _____ in the lunchroom.

Today, my teacher will _____ in a different room.

She _____ with the other teachers.

Yesterday, we _____ pizza, pears, and peas.

Today, we will _____ soup and potatoes.

Leave, Leaves, and Left

We use **leave** and **leaves** to tell about now. We use **left** to tell about what already happened.

Write **leave**, **leaves**, or **left** in the sentences below.

Last winter, we _____ seeds in the bird feeder every day.

My mother likes to _____ food out for the squirrels.

When it rains, she _____ bread for the birds.

Yesterday, she _____ popcorn for the birds.

Learning Dictionary Skills

A dictionary is a book that gives the meanings of words. It also tells how words sound. Words in a dictionary are in ABC order. That makes them easier to find.

Look at this page from a dictionary. Then, answer the questions and color the pictures.

baby
a very young child

band
a group of people who play music

bank
a place where money is kept

bark
the sound a dog makes

berry
a small, juicy fruit

board
a flat piece of wood

What is a small, juicy fruit? _____

What is a group of people who play music? _____

What is the name of a very young child? _____

What is a flat piece of wood called? _____

Learning Dictionary Skills

Look at this page from a dictionary. Then, answer the questions and color the pictures.

safe: a metal box

sea: a body of water

seed: the beginning of a plant

sheep: an animal that has wool

store: a place where items are sold

skate: a shoe with wheels or a blade on it

snowstorm: a time when much snow falls

squirrel: a small animal with a bushy tail

stone: a small rock

What kind of animal has wool? _____

What do you call a shoe with wheels on it? _____

When a lot of snow falls, what is it called? _____

What is a small animal with a bushy tail? _____

What is a place where items are sold? _____

When a plant starts, what is it called? _____

Look at this page from a dictionary. Then, answer the questions and draw something that could come after **tiger** in the dictionary.

table: furniture with legs and a flat top

teacher: a person who teaches lessons

telephone: a device that sends and receives sounds

ticket: a paper slip or card that allows someone to enter an event

tiger: an animal with stripes

Who is a person who teaches lessons? _____

What is the name of an animal with stripes? _____

What is a piece of furniture with legs and a flat top? _____

What is the definition of a ticket?

_____

What is a device that sends
and receives sounds?

_____

Learning Dictionary Skills

The guide words at the top of a page in a dictionary tell you what the first and last words on the page will be. Only words that come in ABC order between those two words will be on that page. Guide words help you find the page you need to look up a word.

Write each word from the box in ABC order between each pair of guide words.

| faint | far | fence | feed | farmer |
| fan | feet | farm | family | face |

face   **fence**

_____   _____

_____   _____

_____   _____

_____   _____

Learning Dictionary Skills

Create your own dictionary page. Include guide words at the top. Write the words with their meanings in ABC order. Then, draw and color a picture of one of the words.

_____
guide word

_____
word
_____
_____

_____
guide word

_____
word
_____
_____

_____
word
_____
_____

_____
word
_____
_____

_____
word
_____
_____

Short a Words: Rhyming Words

Short a is the sound you hear in the word **math**.

Use the **short a** words in the box to write rhyming words. Then, draw a picture of one of the words.

| lamp | math | can | bat | fan | Dan |
| path | fat | stamp | cat | van | sat |

Write four words that rhyme with **mat**.

_____ _____ _____ _____

Write two words that rhyme with **bath**.

_____ _____

Write two words that rhyme with **damp**.

_____ _____

Write four words that rhyme with **pan**.

_____

_____

_____

_____

Long a Words

Long a is a vowel sound that says its own name. **Long a** can be spelled **ai** as in the word **mail**, **ay** as in the word **say**, and **a** with a **silent e** at the end as in the word **same**.

Say each word and listen for the **long a** sound. Then, write each word and underline the letters that make the **long a** vowel sound.

mail	made	play	sale
game	bake	gray	name
paint	day	train	tray

_____   _____

_____   _____

_____   _____

_____   _____

_____   _____

Short e Words

Short e is the vowel sound you hear in the word **pet**.

Say each word and listen for the **short e** sound. Write each word and underline the letter that makes the **short e** sound. Then, draw a picture to show one of the words.

red	pet	test	tent
bed	rest	when	best

_____   _____

_____   _____

_____   _____

_____   _____

Long e Words: Rhyming Words

ong e is the vowel sound you hear in the word **meet**.

Use the **long e** words in the box to write rhyming words. Then, draw a picture to show one of the words.

street	mean	deal	neat	clean	meal
keep	feet	beast	sleep	treat	feast

Write the words that rhyme with **beat**.

_____ _____ _____

Write the words that rhyme with **deep**.

_____ _____

Write the words that rhyme with **feel**.

_____ _____

Write the words that rhyme with **bean**.

_____ _____

Write the words that rhyme with **least**.

_____ _____

Short i Words: Rhyming Words

Short i is the sound you hear in the word **pin**.

Use the **short i** words in the box to write rhyming words. Then, draw a picture to show one of the words.

| pin | ship | wish | win | dish | kick |
| pitch | fin | dip | rich | fish | sick |

Write the words that rhyme with **spin**.

_____   _____   _____

Write the words that rhyme with **squish**.

_____   _____   _____

Write the words that rhyme with **ditch**.

_____   _____

Write the words that rhyme with **rip**.

_____   _____

Write the words that rhyme with **lick**.

_____   _____

Long i Words: Rhyming Words

long i is the sound you hear in the word **fight**.

Use the **long i** words in the box to write rhyming words. Then, draw a picture to show one of the words.

hide	sight	nine	line	my
by	ride	fly	high	light

Write the words that rhyme with **sigh**.

_____   _____   _____   _____

Write the words that rhyme with **side**.

_____   _____

Write the words that rhyme with **fine**.

_____   _____

Write the words that rhyme with **fight**.

_____   _____

© Carson-Dellosa

CD-704891

Short o Words: Rhyming Words

Short o is the vowel sound you hear in the word **got**.

Use the **short o** words in the box to write rhyming words.

hot	**box**	**sock**	**lock**	**clock**	**mop**
stop	**rock**	**mob**	**fox**	**cot**	**Bob**

Write the words that rhyme with **dot**.

_____   _____

Write the words that rhyme with **socks**.

_____   _____

Write the words that rhyme with **hop**.

_____   _____

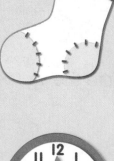

Write the words that rhyme with **dock**.

_____   _____

_____   _____

Write the words that rhyme with **cob**.

_____   _____

Long o Words

Long o is a vowel sound that says its own name. Long o can be spelled oa as in the word **float** or **o** with a **silent e** at the end as in the word **cone**.

Say each word and listen for the **long o** sound. Then, write each word and underline the letters that make the **long o** sound.

rope	coat	soap	wrote
note	hope	boat	cone
bone	pole	phone	hole

_____ _____

_____ _____

_____ _____

_____ _____

_____ _____

_____ _____

© Carson-Dellosa
CD-704891

Short u Words

Short u is the sound you hear in the word **bug**.

Say each word and listen for the **short u** sound. Write each word and underline the letter that makes the **short u** sound. Then, draw a picture to show one of the words.

pump	nut	rug	jump
hug	tub	bug	cub

_____   _____

_____   _____

_____   _____

_____   _____

Long u Words

Long u is a vowel sound which says its own name. **Long u** is spelled **u** with a **silent e** at the end as in **cute**. The letters **oo** make a sound very much like long u. They make the sound you hear in the word **zoo**. The letters **ew** also make the **oo** sound as in the word **grew**.

Say the words and listen for the **u** and **oo** sounds. Write each word and underline the letters that make the **long u** and **oo** sounds. Then, draw a picture to show one of the words.

cube	blew	moon	goose
flew	loose	tooth	fuse

_____   _____

_____   _____

_____   _____

_____   _____

Family Words

Some words tell how a person looks or feels. These are called **describing words** or **adjectives**.

Help Andy write about the people in his family. Write a sentence that uses both describing words in each box.

Example:

funny tall	My aunt is tall and funny .
happy smiling	My grandmother _____ .
hot tired	My uncle _____ .
thirsty hungry	My little brother _____ .

Joining words often join two sentences to make one long sentence. Three words help do this:

and: if both sentences are much the same

Example: I took my dog for a walk, **and** I played with my cat.

but: if the second sentence says something different from the first sentence. Sometimes the second sentence tells why you can't do the first sentence.

Example: I want to play outside, **but** it is raining.

or: if each sentence names a different choice

Example: You could eat your cookie, **or** you could give it to me.

Use the word given to join the two short sentences into one longer sentence.

Example:

but	My aunt lives far away, but she calls me often.
My aunt lives far away. She calls me often.	

and	_____ _____
My sister had a birthday. She got a new bike.	

or	_____ _____
We can play outside. Or we can play inside.	

Location Words

Use one of the location words from the box to complete each sentence. Then, color the pictures.

| between | around | inside | outside | beside | across |

Example:
She will hide _____**under**_____ the basket.

In the summer, we like to play _____ .

She can swim _____ the pool.

Put the bird _____ its cage so it won't fly away.

Sit _____ Bill and me so we can all work together.

Your picture is right _____ mine on the wall.

The bunny hopped _____ the park.

Spelling Concentration Game

Play this game with a friend. Cut out each word card below and on pages 325 and 327. Lay the cards facedown on a flat surface. Take turns turning over two cards at a time. If the cards match, give the pair to your friend. Then, spell the word from memory. If you spelled it correctly, you can keep the pair. If not, put the cards back facedown. When all of the word cards have been matched and spelled correctly, the players count their pairs. Whoever has the most pairs wins.

You can also play this by yourself or with more than one friend!

dust	**light**	**clean**
bump	**dust**	**sleep**
clean	**bump**	**light**
sleep		

This page is blank for the cutting activity on the opposite side.

note	head	write
soap	made	nine
stop	play	grew
clock	stamp	cute
tent	math	choose

This page is blank for the cutting activity on the opposite side.

note	head	write
soap	made	nine
stop	play	grew
clock	stamp	cute
tent	math	choose

This page is blank for the cutting activity on the opposite side.

Opposite Words

Opposites are words that mean very different things. Use the opposite word from the box to complete these sentences.

hard	hot	bottom	quickly	happy
sad	slowly	cold	soft	top

Example:
The gray bag is on _____top_____ and the blue bag is on the __bottom__.

Snow is _____ , but fire is _____ .

A rabbit runs _____ , but a turtle moves _____ .

A bed is _____ , but a floor is _____ .

I feel _____ when my friends come over and _____ when they leave.

Time Words

The time between breakfast and lunch is **morning**.

The time between lunch and dinner is **afternoon**.

The time between dinner and bedtime is **evening**.

Write a time word from the box to complete each sentence. Use each word only once.

| afternoon | evening | morning | today | tomorrow |

What did you eat for breakfast this _____ ?

We came home from school in the _____ .

I help wash the dinner dishes in the _____ .

I feel a little tired _____ .

If I rest tonight, I will feel better _____ .

Answer Key

Grab Bag

Estimate the number of buttons you can pick up with one hand. Write your guess on the first line. Grab a handful of buttons and put them into groups of ten. Fill in each blank. Repeat with the next bag.

Answers will vary.

Estimate: _____   Estimate: _____

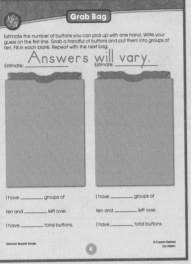

I have _____ groups of   I have _____ groups of

ten and _____ left over.   ten and _____ left over.

I have _____ total buttons.   I have _____ total buttons.

Discover Second Grade   © Carson-Dellosa
                                CD-704891
6

Keeping Score

In the first row, count the balls and make tally marks for each team's goals. In the second row, count the tally marks and write scores for each team.

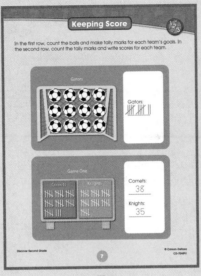

Gators: 𝍷𝍷𝍷 𝍷𝍷𝍷 𝍷𝍷𝍷

Comets: 38

Knights: 35

Discover Second Grade   © Carson-Dellosa
                                CD-704891
7

Keeping Score

In the first row, count the balls and make tally marks for each team's goals. In the second row, count the tally marks and write scores for each team.

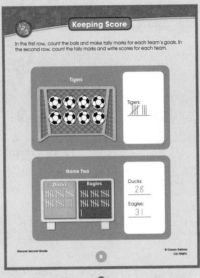

Tigers: 𝍷𝍷𝍷 𝍷𝍷𝍷 𝍷𝍷𝍷

Ducks: 28

Eagles: 31

Discover Second Grade   © Carson-Dellosa
                                CD-704891
8

A Number of Ways

Draw a picture of base ten blocks to show each number. Then, write the number of tens and ones in the blanks.

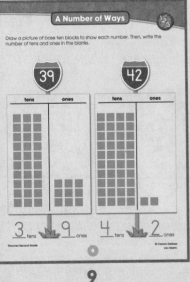

3 tens **9** ones   **4** tens **2** ones

Discover Second Grade   © Carson-Dellosa
                                CD-704891
9

A Number of Ways

Draw a picture of base ten blocks to show each number. Then, write the number of tens and ones in the blanks.

37   24

3 tens **7** ones   **2** tens **4** ones

Discover Second Grade   © Carson-Dellosa
                                CD-704891
10

Expanding Numbers

Write each number in expanded form. The first one has been done for you.

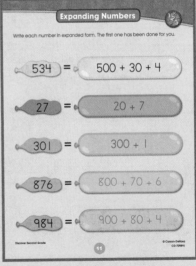

534 = 500 + 30 + 4

27 = 20 + 7

301 = 300 + 1

876 = 800 + 70 + 6

984 = 900 + 80 + 4

Discover Second Grade   © Carson-Dellosa
                                CD-704891
11

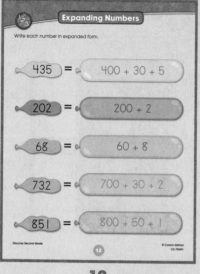

Expanding Numbers

Write each number in expanded form.

435 = 400 + 30 + 5

202 = 200 + 2

68 = 60 + 8

732 = 700 + 30 + 2

851 = 800 + 50 + 1

12

Line Leader

Follow the directions to put the bears in order. Draw and color bears in each box.

- The 1st bear is red.
- The 4th bear is green.
- The 10th bear is blue.
- The 3rd bear is yellow.
- The 2nd and 6th bears are the same color as the 10th bear.

- The 8th and 12th bears are the same color as the 4th bear.
- The 11th and 7th bears are the same color as the 3rd bear.
- The 5th and 9th bears are the same color as the 1st bear.

red | blue | yellow | green | red | blue | yellow | green | red | blue | yellow | green

13

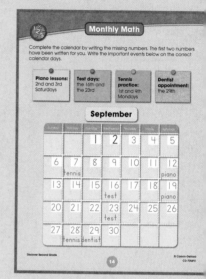

Monthly Math

Complete the calendar by writing the missing numbers. The first two numbers have been written for you. Write the important events below on the correct calendar days.

Piano lessons: 2nd and 3rd Saturdays

Test days: the 16th and the 23rd

Tennis practice: 1st and 4th Mondays

Dentist appointment: the 29th

September

Sunday	Monday	Tuesday	Wednesday	Thursday	Friday	Saturday
		1	2	3	4	5
6	7 tennis	8	9	10	11	12 piano
13	14	15	16 test	17	18	19 piano
20	21	22	23 test	24	25	26
27	28 tennis	29 dentist	30			

14

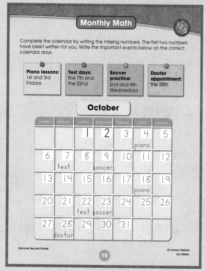

Monthly Math

Complete the calendar by writing the missing numbers. The first two numbers have been written for you. Write the important events below on the correct calendar days.

Piano lessons: 1st and 3rd Fridays

Test days: the 7th and the 22nd

Soccer practice: 2nd and 4th Wednesdays

Doctor appointment: the 28th

October

Sunday	Monday	Tuesday	Wednesday	Thursday	Friday	Saturday
		1	2	3	4 piano	5
6	7 test	8	9 soccer	10	11	12
13	14	15	16	17	18 piano	19
20	21	22 test	23 soccer	24	25	26
27	28 doctor	29	30	31		

15

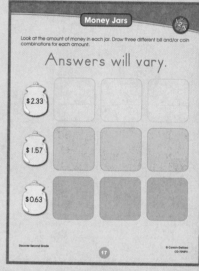

Money Jars

Look at the amount of money in each jar. Draw three different bill and/or coin combinations for each amount.

Answers will vary.

$1.23

$0.78

$2.17

16

Money Jars

Look at the amount of money in each jar. Draw three different bill and/or coin combinations for each amount.

Answers will vary.

$2.33

$1.57

$0.63

17

Answer Key

Money Jars

Look at the amount of money in each jar. Draw three different bill and/or coin combinations for each amount.

Answers will vary.

$1.46

$0.88

$2.71

18

Unlock the Code

Follow the clues to figure out the code number for each lock.

My ones digit is 6. My tens digit is 1 plus my ones digit. My hundreds digit is 1 less than my ones digit. What number am I?

5 7 6

My ones and hundreds digits are the same. My tens digit is 2 less than my ones digit. My ones digit is 4 + 4. What number am I?

8 6 8

19

Unlock the Code

Follow the clues to figure out the code number for each lock.

My ones digit is 4. My tens digit is 1 plus my ones digit. My hundreds digit is 1 less than my ones digit. What number am I?

3 5 4

My hundreds digit is 6. My ones digit is half of my hundreds digit. Add my hundreds digit and ones digit together to get my tens digit. What number am I?

6 9 3

20

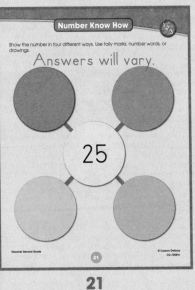

Number Know How

Show the number in four different ways. Use tally marks, number words, or drawings.

Answers will vary.

25

21

Number Know How

Show the number in four different ways. Use tally marks, number words, or drawings.

Answers will vary.

34

22

Write Me a Check!

Write the amount of each check in word form on the line.

Bailey Bug
86 Spotted Highway
Insectville, IZ 3X2Q8   1001

Pay to Lady Beetle Café $718.00

Seven hundred eighteen and 00/100 dollars

For: dinner party   Bailey Bug

Lucy Love
123 Heart Road
Valentine, LU 2W8Q6   1002

Pay to Heartland Formal Wear $190.00

One hundred ninety and 00/100 dollars

For: wedding dress   Lucy Love

23

Discover Second Grade

© Carson-Dellosa
CD-704891

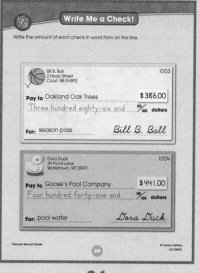

24

25

26

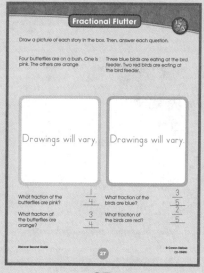

27

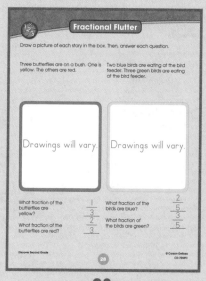

28

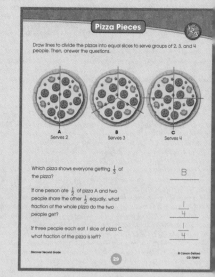

29

Pizza Pieces (30)

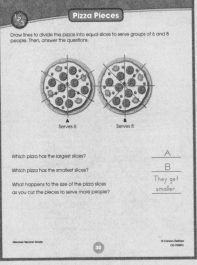

Draw lines to divide the pizzas into equal slices to serve groups of 6 and 8 people. Then, answer the questions.

A Serves 6 **B** Serves 8

Which pizza has the largest slices? — A

Which pizza has the smallest slices? — B

What happens to the size of the pizza slices as you cut the pieces to serve more people? — They get smaller.

30

Make 10! (31)

Drop 10 buttons onto the hand. Count how many of each color you see. Write the numbers in the number sentences. Repeat until you make 6 different combinations that equal 10.

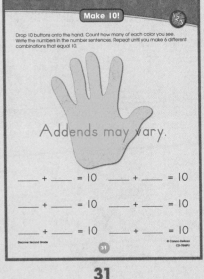

Addends may vary.

____ + ____ = 10   ____ + ____ = 10

____ + ____ = 10   ____ + ____ = 10

____ + ____ = 10   ____ + ____ = 10

31

Make 20! (32)

Drop 20 buttons onto the hand. Count how many of each color you see. Write the numbers in the number sentences. Repeat until you make 6 different combinations that equal 20.

Addends may vary.

____ + ____ = 20   ____ + ____ = 20

____ + ____ = 20   ____ + ____ = 20

____ + ____ = 20   ____ + ____ = 20

32

Find the 10s (33)

Circle the two numbers in each row that equal 10. Then, write the third number in the number sentence with 10 and solve for the sum. The first one has been done for you.

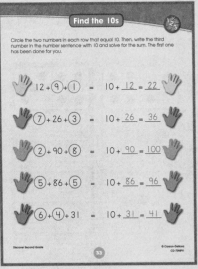

12 + ⑨ + ① = 10 + 12 = 22

⑦ + 26 + ③ = 10 + 26 = 36

② + 90 + ⑧ = 10 + 90 = 100

⑤ + 86 + ⑤ = 10 + 86 = 96

⑥ + ④ + 31 = 10 + 31 = 41

33

Find the 20s (34)

Circle the two numbers in each row that equal 20. Then, write the third number in the number sentence with 20 and solve for the sum. The first one has been done for you.

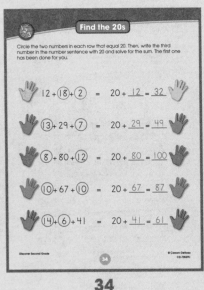

12 + ⑱ + ② = 20 + 12 = 32

⑬ + 29 + ⑦ = 20 + 29 = 49

⑧ + 80 + ⑫ = 20 + 80 = 100

⑩ + 67 + ⑩ = 20 + 67 = 87

⑭ + ⑥ + 41 = 20 + 41 = 61

34

Addition Breakdown (35)

Add each pair of numbers by breaking the second number into tens and ones. Then, add the groups of ten and add the ones. The first two have been started for you.

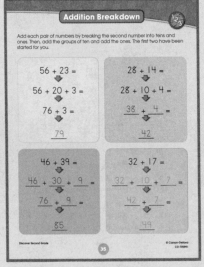

56 + 23 =
56 + 20 + 3 =
76 + 3 =
79

28 + 14 =
28 + 10 + 4 =
38 + 4 =
42

46 + 39 =
46 + 30 + 9 =
76 + 9 =
85

32 + 17 =
32 + 10 + 7 =
42 + 7 =
49

35

36

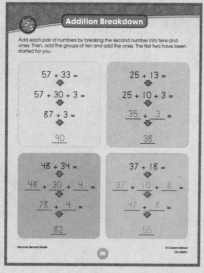

Addition Breakdown

Add each pair of numbers by breaking the second number into tens and ones. Then, add the groups of ten and add the ones. The first two have been started for you.

57 + 33 =
57 + 30 + 3 =
87 + 3 =
90

25 + 13 =
25 + 10 + 3 =
35 + **3** =
38

48 + 34 =
48 + **30** + **4** =
78 + **4** =
82

37 + 18 =
37 + **10** + **8** =
47 + **8** =
55

Discover Second Grade   © Carson-Dellosa CD-704891

37

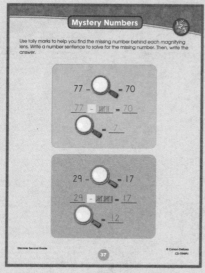

Mystery Numbers

Use tally marks to help you find the missing number behind each magnifying lens. Write a number sentence to solve for the missing number. Then, write the answer.

77 – 〇 = 70
77 – 卌 || = **70**
〇 = **7**

29 – 〇 = 17
29 – 卌 卌 || = **17**
〇 = **12**

Discover Second Grade   © Carson-Dellosa CD-704891

38

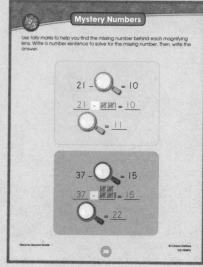

Mystery Numbers

Use tally marks to help you find the missing number behind each magnifying lens. Write a number sentence to solve for the missing number. Then, write the answer.

21 – 〇 = 10
21 – 卌 卌 | = **10**
〇 = **11**

37 – 〇 = 15
37 – 卌 卌 卌 || = **15**
〇 = **22**

Discover Second Grade   © Carson-Dellosa CD-704891

39

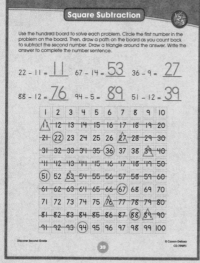

Square Subtraction

Use the hundred board to solve each problem. Circle the first number in the problem on the board. Then, draw a path on the board as you count back to subtract the second number. Draw a triangle around the answer. Write the answer to complete the number sentence.

22 – 11 = **11**   67 – 14 = **53**   36 – 9 = **27**

88 – 12 = **76**   94 – 5 = **89**   51 – 12 = **39**

1	2	3	4	5	6	7	8	9	10
11	12	13	14	15	16	17	18	19	20
21	22	23	24	25	26	27	28	29	30
31	32	33	34	35	36	37	38	39	40
41	42	43	44	45	46	47	48	49	50
51	52	53	54	55	56	57	58	59	60
61	62	63	64	65	66	67	68	69	70
71	72	73	74	75	76	77	78	79	80
81	82	83	84	85	86	87	88	89	90
91	92	93	94	95	96	97	98	99	100

Discover Second Grade   © Carson-Dellosa CD-704891

40

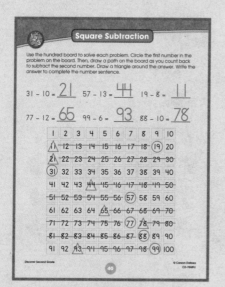

Square Subtraction

Use the hundred board to solve each problem. Circle the first number in the problem on the board. Then, draw a path on the board as you count back to subtract the second number. Draw a triangle around the answer. Write the answer to complete the number sentence.

31 – 10 = **21**   57 – 13 = **44**   19 – 8 = **11**

77 – 12 = **65**   99 – 6 = **93**   88 – 10 = **78**

1	2	3	4	5	6	7	8	9	10
11	12	13	14	15	16	17	18	19	20
21	22	23	24	25	26	27	28	29	30
31	32	33	34	35	36	37	38	39	40
41	42	43	44	45	46	47	48	49	50
51	52	53	54	55	56	57	58	59	60
61	62	63	64	65	66	67	68	69	70
71	72	73	74	75	76	77	78	79	80
81	82	83	84	85	86	87	88	89	90
91	92	93	94	95	96	97	98	99	100

Discover Second Grade   © Carson-Dellosa CD-704891

41

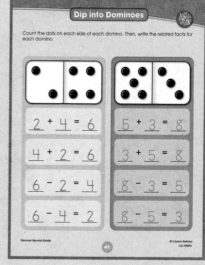

Dip into Dominoes

Count the dots on each side of each domino. Then, write the related facts for each domino.

2 + 4 = 6
4 + 2 = 6
6 – 2 = 4
6 – 4 = 2

5 + 3 = 8
3 + 5 = 8
8 – 3 = 5
8 – 5 = 3

Discover Second Grade   © Carson-Dellosa CD-704891

Answer Key

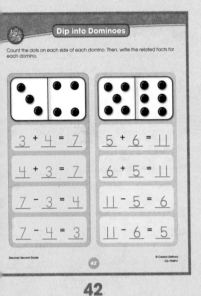

42

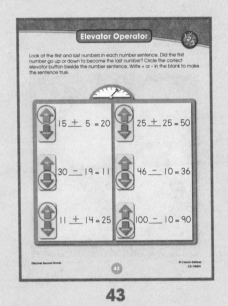

43

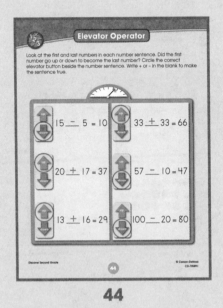

44

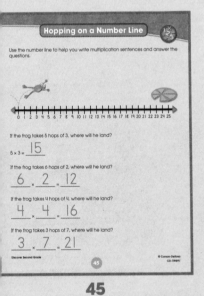

45

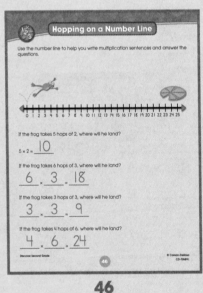

46

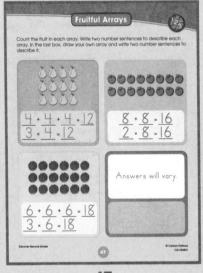

47

© Carson-Dellosa

CD-704891

Answer Key

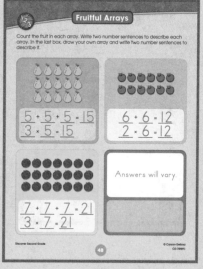

Fruitful Arrays

Count the fruit in each array. Write two number sentences to describe each array. In the last box, draw your own array and write two number sentences to describe it.

$5 + 5 + 5 = 15$
$3 \times 5 = 15$

$6 + 6 = 12$
$2 \times 6 = 12$

$7 + 7 + 7 = 21$
$3 \times 7 = 21$

Answers will vary.

48

The Great Divide

Show 4 ways that you can divide 20 pennies into equal groups. Draw each way on a planet.

Answers will vary.

49

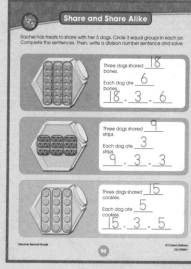

Share and Share Alike

Rachel has treats to share with her 3 dogs. Circle 3 equal groups in each jar. Complete the sentences. Then, write a division number sentence and solve.

Three dogs shared __18__ bones.
Each dog ate __6__ bones.
$18 \div 3 = 6$

Three dogs shared __9__ strips.
Each dog ate __3__ strips.
$9 \div 3 = 3$

Three dogs shared __15__ cookies.
Each dog ate __5__ cookies.
$15 \div 3 = 5$

50

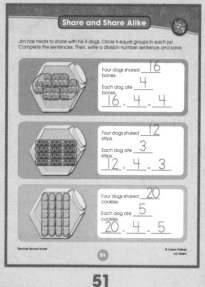

Share and Share Alike

Jim has treats to share with his 4 dogs. Circle 4 equal groups in each jar. Complete the sentences. Then, write a division number sentence and solve.

Four dogs shared __16__ bones.
Each dog ate __4__ bones.
$16 \div 4 = 4$

Four dogs shared __12__ strips.
Each dog ate __3__ strips.
$12 \div 4 = 3$

Four dogs shared __20__ cookies.
Each dog ate __5__ cookies.
$20 \div 4 = 5$

51

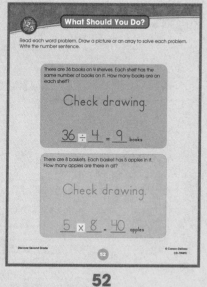

What Should You Do?

Read each word problem. Draw a picture or an array to solve each problem. Write the number sentence.

There are 36 books on 4 shelves. Each shelf has the same number of books on it. How many books are on each shelf?

Check drawing.

$36 \div 4 = 9$ books

There are 8 baskets. Each basket has 5 apples in it. How many apples are there in all?

Check drawing.

$5 \times 8 = 40$ apples

52

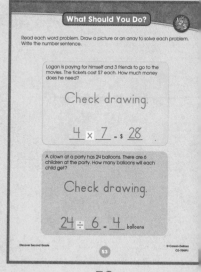

What Should You Do?

Read each word problem. Draw a picture or an array to solve each problem. Write the number sentence.

Logan is paying for himself and 3 friends to go to the movies. The tickets cost $7 each. How much money does he need?

Check drawing.

$4 \times 7 = \$ 28$

A clown at a party has 24 balloons. There are 6 children at the party. How many balloons will each child get?

Check drawing.

$24 \div 6 = 4$ balloons

53

Answer Key

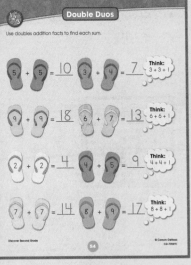

Double Duos

Use doubles addition facts to find each sum.

$5 + 5 = 10$ $3 + 4 = 7$ **Think:** $3 + 3 + 1$

$9 + 9 = 18$ $6 + 7 = 13$ **Think:** $6 + 6 + 1$

$2 + 2 = 4$ $4 + 5 = 9$ **Think:** $4 + 4 + 1$

$7 + 7 = 14$ $8 + 9 = 17$ **Think:** $8 + 8 + 1$

54

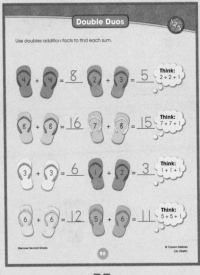

Double Duos

Use doubles addition facts to find each sum.

$4 + 4 = 8$ $2 + 3 = 5$ **Think:** $2 + 2 + 1$

$8 + 8 = 16$ $7 + 8 = 15$ **Think:** $7 + 7 + 1$

$3 + 3 = 6$ $1 + 2 = 3$ **Think:** $1 + 1 + 1$

$6 + 6 = 12$ $5 + 6 = 11$ **Think:** $5 + 5 + 1$

55

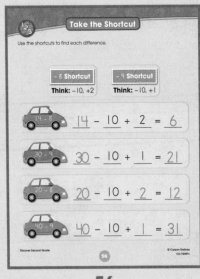

Take the Shortcut

Use the shortcuts to find each difference.

- 8 Shortcut Think: $-10, +2$ **- 9 Shortcut** Think: $-10, +1$

$14 - 8$ $14 - 10 + 2 = 6$

$30 - 9$ $30 - 10 + 1 = 21$

$20 - 8$ $20 - 10 + 2 = 12$

$40 - 9$ $40 - 10 + 1 = 31$

56

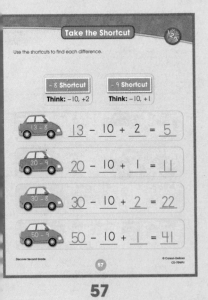

Take the Shortcut

Use the shortcuts to find each difference.

- 8 Shortcut Think: $-10, +2$ **- 9 Shortcut** Think: $-10, +1$

$13 - 8$ $13 - 10 + 2 = 5$

$20 - 9$ $20 - 10 + 1 = 11$

$30 - 8$ $30 - 10 + 2 = 22$

$50 - 9$ $50 - 10 + 1 = 41$

57

The Estimation Shop

You have $1.00. Estimate to find out if you have enough money to buy the items listed. Use coins to check your answers. Then, circle yes or no.

60¢ 69¢ 75¢ 25¢ 88¢ 65¢ 15¢

Do you have enough to buy a yo-yo and a top? **no**

Do you have enough to buy a toy train and a toy sailboat? **yes**

Do you have enough to buy a ball and a teddy bear? **no**

Do you have enough to buy a pencil and a toy sailboat? **yes**

58

The Estimation Shop

You have $1.25. Estimate to find out if you have enough money to buy the items listed. Use coins to check your answers. Then, circle yes or no.

70¢ 79¢ 95¢ 35¢ 99¢ 50¢ 20¢

Do you have enough to buy a toy train and a pencil? **yes**

Do you have enough to buy a toy train and a yo-yo? **no**

Do you have enough to buy a ball and a toy sailboat? **no**

Do you have enough to buy a pencil and a yo-yo? **yes**

59

Answer Key

Brain Power

Use mental math to find each sum. (Hint: Make tens or multiples of 10 first.) Then, write in the cloud how you solved each problem.

Answers will vary.

$12 + 5 + 8 + 5 = 30$

$31 + 7 + 3 = 41$

$7 + 9 + 13 = 29$

$80 + 19 + 1 = 100$

60

Brain Power

Use mental math to find each sum. (Hint: Make tens or multiples of 10 first.) Then, write in the cloud how you solved each problem.

Answers will vary.

$13 + 4 + 7 + 4 = 28$

$41 + 8 + 2 = 51$

$8 + 7 + 14 = 29$

$70 + 18 + 3 = 91$

61

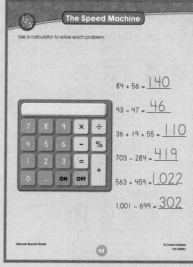

The Speed Machine

Use a calculator to solve each problem.

$84 + 56 = 140$

$93 - 47 = 46$

$36 + 19 + 55 = 110$

$703 - 284 = 419$

$563 + 459 = 1,022$

$1,001 - 699 = 302$

62

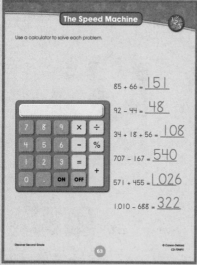

The Speed Machine

Use a calculator to solve each problem.

$85 + 66 = 151$

$92 - 44 = 48$

$34 + 18 + 56 = 108$

$707 - 167 = 540$

$571 + 455 = 1,026$

$1,010 - 688 = 322$

63

Clothing Sort

Sort and classify the clothing into groups. Then, on a separate sheet of paper, write how you classified each group.

Answers will vary.

64

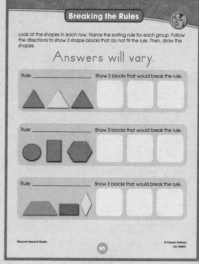

Breaking the Rules

Look at the shapes in each row. Name the sorting rule for each group. Follow the directions to show 3 shape blocks that do not fit the rule. Then, draw the shapes.

Answers will vary.

Rule: _____   Show 3 blocks that would break the rule.

Rule: _____   Show 3 blocks that would break the rule.

Rule: _____   Show 3 blocks that would break the rule.

65

Answer Key

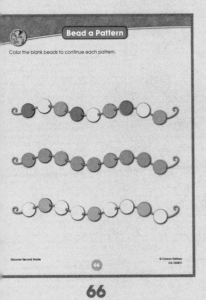

Bead a Pattern

Color the blank beads to continue each pattern.

66

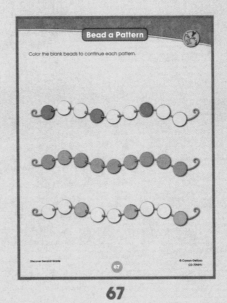

Bead a Pattern

Color the blank beads to continue each pattern.

67

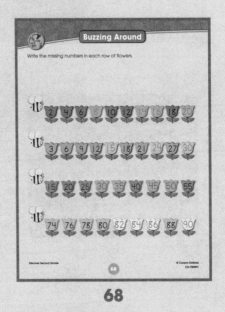

Buzzing Around

Write the missing numbers in each row of flowers.

2 4 6 8 10 12 14 16 18 20

3 6 9 12 15 18 21 24 27 30

15 20 25 30 35 40 45 50 55

74 76 78 80 82 84 86 88 90

68

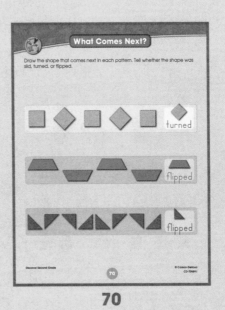

Buzzing Around

Write the missing numbers in each row of flowers.

1 3 5 7 9 11 13 15 17 19

10 12 14 16 18 20 22 24 26 28

5 10 15 20 25 30 35 40 45

64 66 68 70 72 74 76 78 80

69

What Comes Next?

Draw the shape that comes next in each pattern. Tell whether the shape was slid, turned, or flipped.

turned

flipped

flipped

70

Out of This World Patterns

Look at the rules and number patterns. Write the missing rules and numbers.

Rule: +7   7 14 21 28 35 42 49 56

Rule: −2   19 17 15 13 11 9 7 5

Rule: −3   28 25 22 19 16 13 10 7 4

Rule: −5   85 80 75 70 65 60 55 50

71

72

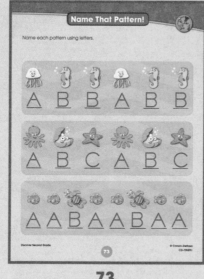

73

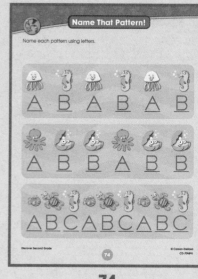

74

75

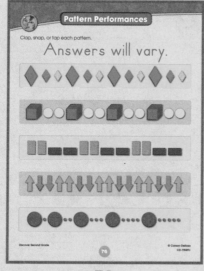

76

77

Answer Key

What Repeats?

Name each pattern using letters. Circle the repeating parts in each letter pattern. Then, create a matching pattern by drawing circles and squares.

A A B A A B A A B

Answers will vary.

A B B A B B A B B

Answers will vary.

Discover Second Grade

78

© Carson-Dellosa
CD-704891

78

Bucket of Buttons

Each child named the button pattern in a different way. Explain each child's rule.

A B C A B C A B C

Explain Jayla's rule: _big button, medium button, small button_

A B A A B A A B A

Explain Carson's rule: _blue button, red button, blue button_

A A B A A B A A B

Explain Nina's rule: _4-hole button, 4-hole button, 2-hole button_

Discover Second Grade

79

© Carson-Dellosa
CD-704891

79

What's the Rule?

Draw what comes next in each pattern.

Discover Second Grade

80

© Carson-Dellosa
CD-704891

80

Growing Shapes

Draw what comes next in each pattern.

Discover Second Grade

81

© Carson-Dellosa
CD-704891

81

Missing Pieces

Draw the missing sets in each pattern.

Discover Second Grade

82

© Carson-Dellosa
CD-704891

82

True or False?

Decide if each statement is true or false. Circle T for true or F for false.

If $3 + 4 = 7$, then $4 + 3 = 7$. (T) F

If $20 + 0 = 20$, then $0 + 20 = 20$. (T) F

If $3 + 4 + 4 + 2 = 13$, then
$13 = 2 + 4 + 4 + 3$. (T) F

If $12 - 0 = 12$, then $0 - 12 = 12$. T (F)

If $23 + 50 = 73$, then $73 = 50 + 23$. (T) F

If $18 - 9 = 9$, then $9 = 9 - 18$. T (F)

Discover Second Grade

83

© Carson-Dellosa
CD-704891

83

Answer Key

84 — True or False?

Decide if each statement is true or false. Circle T for true or F for false.

If 3 + 5 = 8, then 5 + 3 = 8.	(T)	F
If 30 + 0 = 30, then 0 + 30 = 30.	(T)	F
If 2 + 3 + 3 + 5 = 13, then 13 = 5 + 3 + 3 + 2.	(T)	F
If 13 – 0 = 13, then 0 – 13 = 13.	T	(F)
If 33 + 60 = 93, then 93 = 60 + 33.	(T)	F
If 17 – 8 = 9, then 17 – 9 = 8.	(T)	F

84

85 — Symbol Substitute

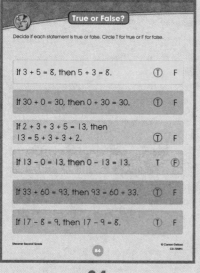

Figure out the missing number behind each picture. Then, write the number.

40 + ◯ = 50   ◯ = 10

🍃 – 70 = 20   🍃 = 90

10 + ⭐ = 30   ⭐ = 20

80 – 🎈 = 20   🎈 = 60

85

86 — Symbol Substitute

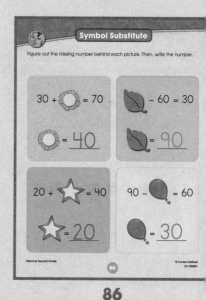

Figure out the missing number behind each picture. Then, write the number.

30 + ◯ = 70   ◯ = 40

🍃 – 60 = 30   🍃 = 90

20 + ⭐ = 40   ⭐ = 20

90 – 🎈 = 60   🎈 = 30

86

87 — Greater Than, Less Than

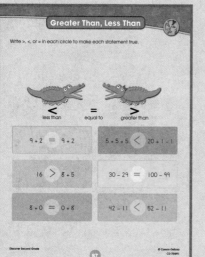

Write >, <, or = in each circle to make each statement true.

less than < | equal to = | greater than >

9 + 2 = 9 + 2	5 + 5 + 5 < 20 + 1 – 1
16 > 8 + 5	30 – 29 = 100 – 99
8 + 0 = 0 + 8	42 – 11 < 52 – 11

87

88 — Greater Than, Less Than

Write >, <, or = in each circle to make each statement true.

less than < | equal to = | greater than >

8 + 1 < 10 + 11	6 + 6 + 6 = 20 – 1 – 1
17 = 8 + 9	60 – 59 = 99 – 98
9 + 0 = 0 + 9	33 – 11 < 44 – 11

88

89 — Mystery Machines

Write the missing numbers and rules for each machine.

Machine 1: RULE: +10
IN	OUT
8	18
24	34
33	43
17	27
61	71

Machine 2: RULE: –5
IN	OUT
100	95
54	49
17	12
99	94
5	0

Machine 3: RULE: –3
IN	OUT
84	81
22	19
4	1
46	43
15	12

Machine 4: RULE: +7
IN	OUT
21	28
14	21
28	35
1	8
56	63

89

Mystery Machines

Write the missing numbers and rules for each machine.

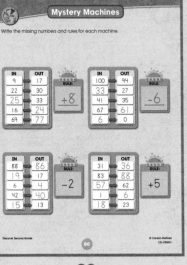

90

Count Up and Back

Follow the rules in each box. Write the missing number on each object.

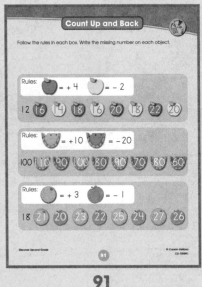

91

Count Up and Back

Follow the rules in each box. Write the missing number on each object.

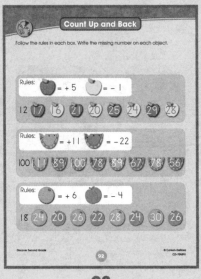

92

What's the Weather?

Read the temperatures on Monday's weather map. Then, read the temperatures on Tuesday's weather map. Write the temperatures for each city. Then, record the difference in temperature for each city.

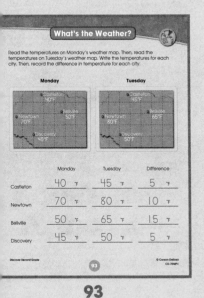

	Monday	Tuesday	Difference
Castleton	40 °F	45 °F	5 °F
Newtown	70 °F	80 °F	10 °F
Bellville	50 °F	65 °F	15 °F
Discovery	45 °F	50 °F	5 °F

93

What's the Weather?

Read the temperatures on Friday's weather map. Then, read the temperatures on Saturday's weather map. Write the temperatures for each city. Then, record the difference in temperature for each city.

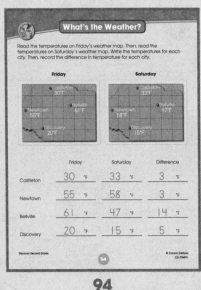

	Friday	Saturday	Difference
Castleton	30 °F	33 °F	3 °F
Newtown	55 °F	58 °F	3 °F
Bellville	61 °F	47 °F	14 °F
Discovery	20 °F	15 °F	5 °F

94

Create a Shape

Use the pattern block of each shape to draw two larger figures. One example has been done for you.

Answers will vary.

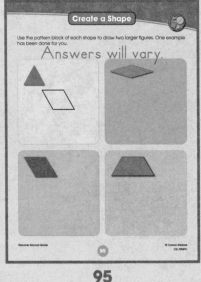

95

Answer Key

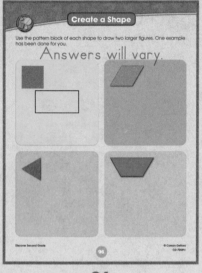

96

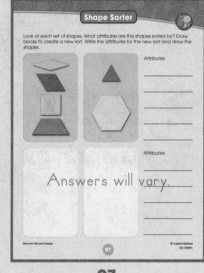

97

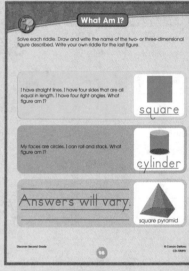

98

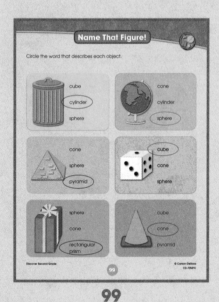

99

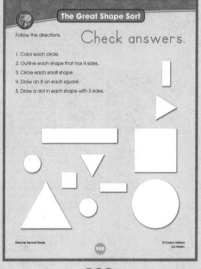

100

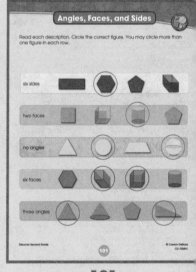

101

Answer Key

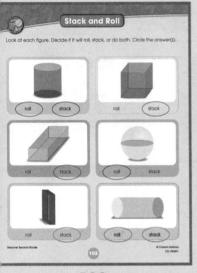

102

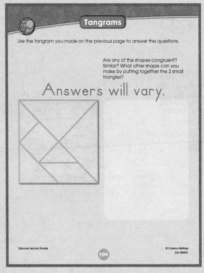

103

104

105

106

107

108

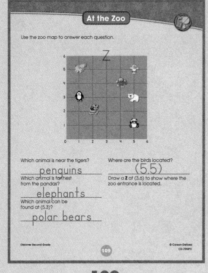

109

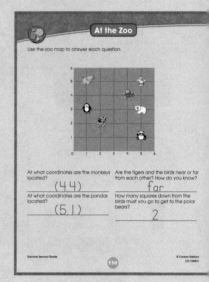

110

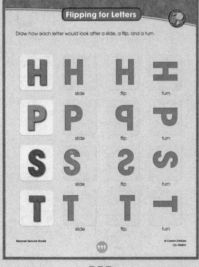

111

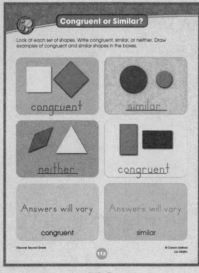

112

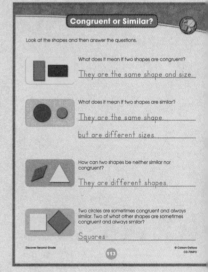

113

Answer Key

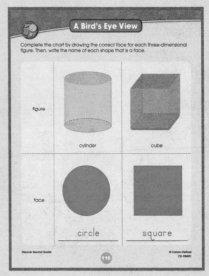

114

115

116

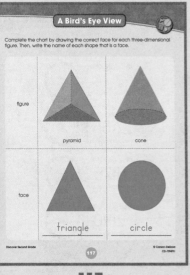

117

118

119

I Spy Shapes

Look around the room for objects that have shapes like those in the picture below. Find at least two objects that are each type of shape. Circle the shapes below when you find them.

Answers will vary.

120

Time Will Tell

Circle the unit of time you would use to measure each activity. Then, write the order of the units of time from 1 to 6, with 1 being the shortest unit of time.

brush your teeth — (minutes) hours — 2
take a vacation — minutes (days) — 4
build a house — hours (months) — 5
grow a tree — (years) days — 6
tie your shoes — (seconds) minutes — 1
bake a cake — (hours) weeks — 3

121

Time and Time Again

Read the times. Draw the hands and write the numbers for each time given.

five o'clock — 5:00
three thirty — 3:30
quarter after one — 1:15
quarter to six — 5:45
seven o'clock — 7:00
five minutes after two — 2:05

122

The Hands of Time

Draw the hands to show the time. Repeat for each clock.

12:05
7:10
3:30
10:15

123

The Hands of Time

Write the numbers to show the time. Repeat for each clock.

6:15
9:05
4:45
8:35

124

The Hands of Time

Draw the hands to show the time. Repeat for each clock.

1:10
7:55
4:25
2:40

125

Answer Key

126

127

128

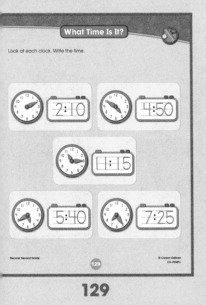

129

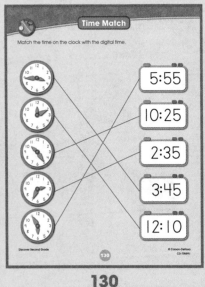

130

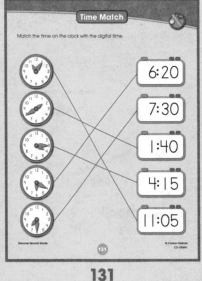

131

132

133

134

135

136

137

138

Penny Counts

Measure the length of each object with pennies. Write the measurement on the line.

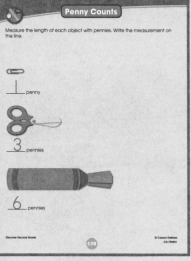

1 penny

3 pennies

6 pennies

138

Penny Counts

Measure the length of each object with pennies. Write the measurement on the line.

4 pennies

5 pennies

2 pennies

139

Buggy About Measurement

Measure the length of each bug with paper clips. Write the measurement on the line.

Answers will vary.

The ladybug is about _____ paper clip(s) long.

The bee is about _____ paper clip(s) long.

140

Buggy About Measurement

Measure the length of the butterfly with paper clips. Write the measurement on the line.

Answers will vary.

The butterfly is about _____ paper clips long.

141

Measure Up!

Estimate the length of a desk or a table. Then, measure it with each item.

Answers will vary.

Estimate: _____ paper clips long
Actual: _____ paper clips long

Estimate: _____ pencils long
Actual: _____ pencils long

Estimate: _____ paintbrushes long
Actual: _____ paintbrushes long

Estimate: _____ scissors long
Actual: _____ scissors long

142

Ribbon Measurement

Use the width of your thumb to measure the length of each ribbon.

Answers will vary.

_____ thumbs long

_____ thumbs long

_____ thumbs long

_____ thumbs long

_____ thumbs long

143

Answer Key

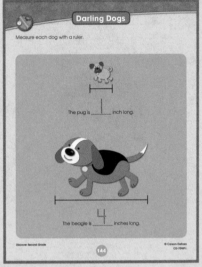

Darling Dogs

Measure each dog with a ruler.

The pug is ___1___ inch long.

The beagle is ___4___ inches long.

Discover Second Grade

© Carson-Dellosa
CD-70489

144

144

Darling Dogs

Measure each dog with a ruler.

The poodle is ___2___ inches long.

The dachshund is ___6___ inches long.

Discover Second Grade

© Carson-Dellosa
CD-70489

145

145

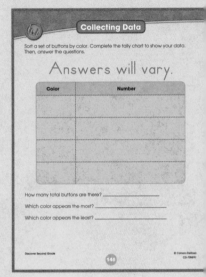

Collecting Data

Sort a set of buttons by color. Complete the tally chart to show your data. Then, answer the questions.

Answers will vary.

Color	Number

How many total buttons are there? _____

Which color appears the most? _____

Which color appears the least? _____

Discover Second Grade

© Carson-Dellosa
CD-70489

146

146

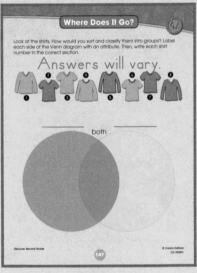

Where Does It Go?

Look at the shirts. How would you sort and classify them into groups? Label each side of the Venn diagram with an attribute. Then, write each shirt number in the correct section.

Answers will vary.

both

Discover Second Grade

© Carson-Dellosa
CD-70489

147

147

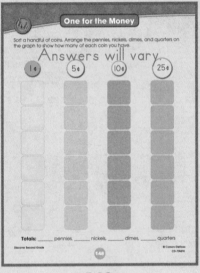

One for the Money

Sort a handful of coins. Arrange the pennies, nickels, dimes, and quarters on the graph to show how many of each coin you have.

Answers will vary.

1¢   5¢   10¢   25¢

Totals: _____ pennies, _____ nickels, _____ dimes, _____ quarters

Discover Second Grade

© Carson-Dellosa
CD-70489

148

148

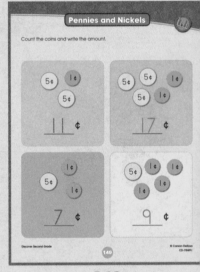

Pennies and Nickels

Count the coins and write the amount.

5¢ 1¢ 5¢   ___11___ ¢

5¢ 5¢ 1¢ 5¢ 1¢   ___17___ ¢

5¢ 1¢ 1¢   ___7___ ¢

5¢ 1¢ 1¢ 1¢ 1¢   ___9___ ¢

Discover Second Grade

© Carson-Dellosa
CD-70489

149

149

Answer Key

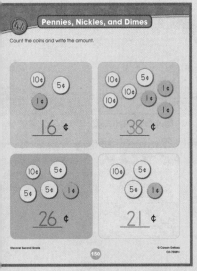

Pennies, Nickles, and Dimes

Count the coins and write the amount.

16 ¢   38 ¢

26 ¢   21 ¢

150

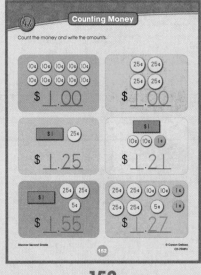

Toy Store

Draw a line from the toy to the amount of money it costs.

36¢
68¢
43¢
57¢
22¢

151

Counting Money

Count the money and write the amounts.

$ 1.00 $ 1.00

$ 1.25 $ 1.21

$ 1.55 $ 1.27

152

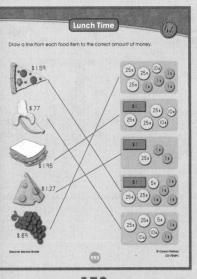

Lunch Time

Draw a line from each food item to the correct amount of money.

$1.59
$.77
$1.95
$1.27
$.89

153

Preferred Pets

Look at the results of a class survey about favorite pets. Draw smiley faces to show the data in a pictograph. Look at the key to see how many votes each smiley face stands for.

= 2 votes

154

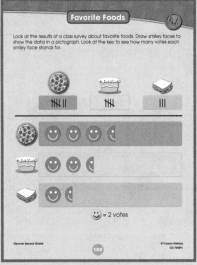

Favorite Foods

Look at the results of a class survey about favorite foods. Draw smiley faces to show the data in a pictograph. Look at the key to see how many votes each smiley face stands for.

= 2 votes

155

© Carson-Dellosa
CD-704891

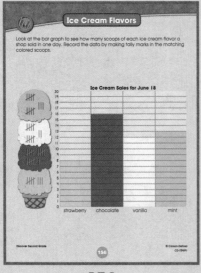

156

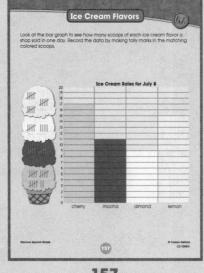

157

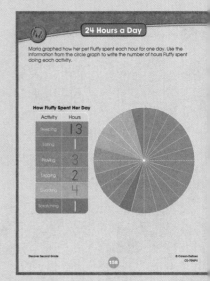

158

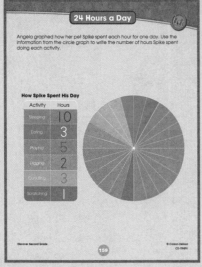

159

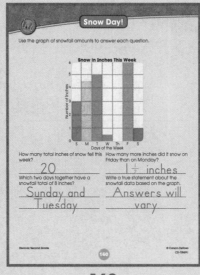

160

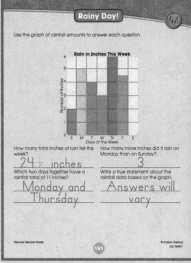

161

Answer Key

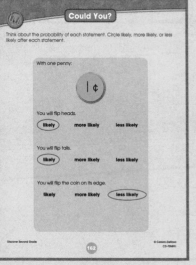

162

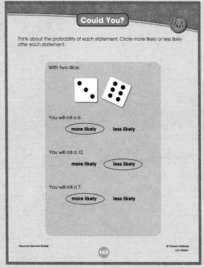

163

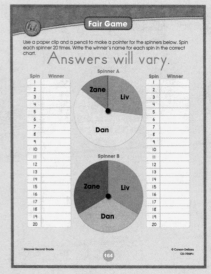

164

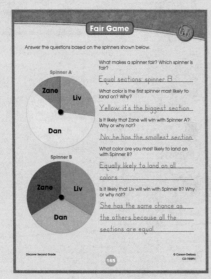

165

166

168

All About Me!

Fill in the blanks to tell all about you! Answers will vary.

Name _____
      (First)   (Last)
Address _____
City _____
State _____
Phone number _____
Age _____

Places I have visited: _____
_____
_____

My favorite vacation: _____
_____
_____

169

Beginning Consonants: b, c, d, f, g, h, j

Fill in the beginning consonant for each word. Then, color the pictures.

Example: __c__ at

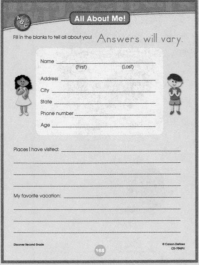

__b__ ag

__f__ ish

__g__ oat

__h__ orse

__d__ og

__j__ ellyfish

170

Beginning Consonants: k, l, m, n, p, q, r

Fill in the beginning consonant for each word. Then, color the pictures.

Example: __r__ ibbon

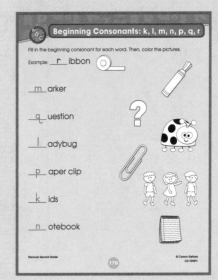

__m__ arker

__q__ uestion

__l__ adybug

__p__ aper clip

__k__ ids

__n__ otebook

171

Beginning Consonants: s, t, v, w, y, z

Fill in the beginning consonant for each word. Then, color the pictures.

Example: __s__ cissors

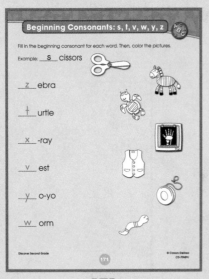

__z__ ebra

__t__ urtle

__x__ -ray

__v__ est

__y__ o-yo

__w__ orm

172

Ending Consonants: b, d, f, g

Fill in the ending consonant for each word. Then, draw and color a picture of something else that ends with **b**, **d**, **f**, or **g**.

pyrami __d__

scar __f__

ladybu __g__

bir __d__

cra __b__

Drawings will vary.

173

Ending Consonants: k, l, m, n, p, r

Fill in the ending consonant for each word. Then, draw and color a picture of something else that ends with **k**, **l**, **m**, **n**, **p**, or **r**.

balloo __n__

ar __m__

dinne __r__

des __k__

paper cli __p__

cerea __l__

Drawings will vary.

174

Ending Consonants: s, t, x

Fill in the ending consonant for each word. Then, draw and color a picture of something else that ends with **s**, **t**, or **x**.

elephan **t**

bo **x**

bu **s**

hear **t**

ne **t**

Drawings will vary.

Discover Second Grade — 174 — © Carson-Dellosa CD-704891

175

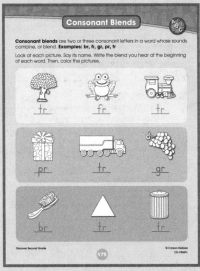

Consonant Blends

Consonant blends are two or three consonant letters in a word whose sounds combine, or blend. **Examples: br, fr, gr, pr, tr**

Look at each picture. Say its name. Write the blend you hear at the beginning of each word. Then, color the pictures.

tr — **fr** — **tr**

pr — **tr** — **gr**

br — **tr** — **tr**

Discover Second Grade — 175 — © Carson-Dellosa CD-704891

176

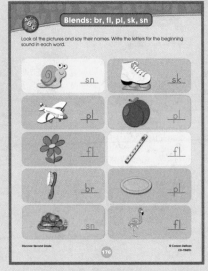

Blends: br, fl, pl, sk, sn

Look at the pictures and say their names. Write the letters for the beginning sound in each word.

sn — **sk**

pl — **pl**

fl — **fl**

br — **pl**

sn — **fl**

Discover Second Grade — 176 — © Carson-Dellosa CD-704891

177

Blends: bl, cl, cr, sl

Look at the pictures and say their names. Write the letters for the beginning sound in each word. Then, color the pictures.

cr ayon — **bl** anket — **cr** acker

cl ock — **bl** ock — **cl** oud

sl ed — **cr** ab — **cl** am

Discover Second Grade — 177 — © Carson-Dellosa CD-704891

178

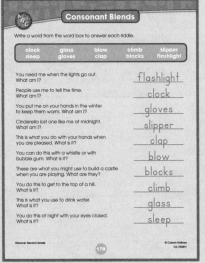

Consonant Blends

Write a word from the word box to answer each riddle.

| clock | glass | blow | climb | slipper |
| sleep | gloves | clap | blocks | flashlight |

You need me when the lights go out. What am I? — flashlight

People use me to tell the time. What am I? — clock

You put me on your hands in the winter to keep them warm. What am I? — gloves

Cinderella lost one like me at midnight. What am I? — slipper

This is what you do with your hands when you are pleased. What is it? — clap

You can do this with a whistle or with bubble gum. What is it? — blow

These are what you might use to build a castle when you are playing. What are they? — blocks

You do this to get to the top of a hill. What is it? — climb

This is what you use to drink water. What is it? — glass

You do this at night with your eyes closed. What is it? — sleep

Discover Second Grade — 178 — © Carson-Dellosa CD-704891

179

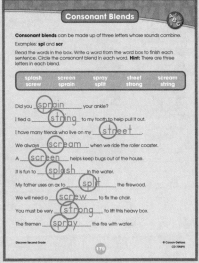

Consonant Blends

Consonant blends can be made up of three letters whose sounds combine.

Examples: **spl** and **scr**

Read the words in the box. Write a word from the word box to finish each sentence. Circle the consonant blend in each word. **Hint:** There are three letters in each blend.

| splash | screen | spray | street | scream |
| screw | sprain | split | strong | string |

Did you **sprain** your ankle?

I tied a **string** to my tooth to help pull it out.

I have many friends who live on my **street**.

We always **scream** when we ride the roller coaster.

A **screen** helps keep bugs out of the house.

It is fun to **splash** in the water.

My father uses an ax to **split** the firewood.

We will need a **screw** to fix the chair.

You must be very **strong** to lift this heavy box.

The firemen **spray** the fire with water.

Discover Second Grade — 179 — © Carson-Dellosa CD-704891

180

Consonant Teams: sh, ch, wh, th

Consonant teams are two or three consonant letters that have a single sound. **Examples: sh** and **tch**

Look at the first picture in each row. Circle the pictures that have the same sound.

wheel — **wh**

shoe — **sh**

chicken — **ch**

181

Consonant Teams

Circle the consonant teams in each word. Use the word box. Write a word from the word box to finish each sentence. Circle the consonant teams in your words. Remember: Consonant teams form one single sound. They are different from blends.

| trash | ship | chair | which | catch |
| shut | splash | when | chain | patch |

My (chair) does not rock.

I put a (chain) on my bike so nobody can take it.

We watched the big (ship) dock and let off its passengers.

It is my job to take out the (trash).

I have to wear a (patch) over my eye until it is better.

The baby likes to (splash) in the bathtub.

Can you (catch) the ball with one hand?

Please (shut) the windows before it rains.

(When) are we going to leave for school?

I don't know (which) of these books is mine.

182

Consonant Blends and Teams

Look at the words in the word box. Write all of the words that end with the **ng** sound in the column under the picture of the **ring**. Write all of the words that end with **nk** sound under the picture of the **junk**. Then, finish the sentences with words from the word box.

| strong | rank | bring | bank | honk | hang | thank |
| long | hunk | song | stung | bunk | sang | junk |

ring — **ng**

strong
long
bring
song
stung
hang
sang

junk — **nk**

rank
hunk
bank
honk
bunk
thank
junk

Honk your horn when you get to my house.

He was _stung_ by a bee.

We are going to put our money in a _bank_.

I want to _thank_ you for the birthday present.

My brother and I sleep in _bunk_ beds.

183

Silent Letters

Some words have letters you can't hear at all, such as the **gh** in **night**, the **w** in **wrong**, the **l** in **walk**, the **k** in **knee**, the **b** in **climb**, and the **t** in **listen**.

Look at the words in the word box. Write the word under its picture. Underline the silent letters. Then, draw and color pictures for the other words.

| knife | light | calf | wrench | lamb | eight |
| night | whistle | comb | thumb | knob | knee |

eight   night   calf

lamb   thumb   Drawings will vary.

184

Hard and Soft c

When **c** is followed by **e, i,** or **y,** it usually has a **soft** sound. The **soft c** sounds like **s**. For example, **c**ircle and fen**c**e. When **c** is followed by **a, o,** or **u,** it usually has a **hard** sound. The **hard c** sounds like **k**.

Example: **c**up and **c**art

Read the words in the word box. Write the words in the correct lists. One word will be in both. Write a word from the word box to finish each sentence.

| pencil | popcorn | tractor | cent | mice |
| dance | candy | cookie | circus | card |

Words with soft c

pencil
dance
cent
mice
circus

Words with hard c

circus
popcorn
candy
tractor
cookie
card

Another word for a penny is a _cent_.

A cat likes to chase _mice_.

You will see animals and clowns at the _circus_.

Will you please sharpen my _pencil_?

185

Hard and Soft c and g

When **g** is followed by **e, i,** or **y,** it usually has a **soft** sound. The **soft g** sounds like **j**.

Example: chan**g**e and **g**entle   When **g** is followed by **a, o,** or **u,** it usually has a hard sound, like the **g** in **g**o or **g**ate.

Look at the **c** and **g** words at the bottom of the page. Cut them out and glue them in the correct box below.

Soft sounds		Hard sounds	
juice	age	grass	jug
gem	giant	crayon	cart
face	engine	goat	grow

Answer Key

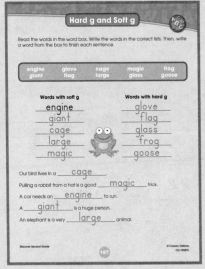

187

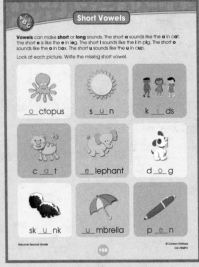

188

189

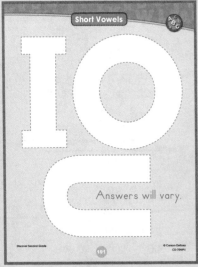

191

193

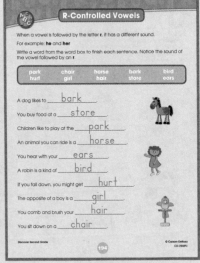

194

R-Controlled Words

R-controlled vowel words are words in which the **r** that comes after the vowel changes the sound of the vowel.

For example: bird, star, burn

Write the correct word in the sentences below.

| horse | jar | dirt | purple | bird | turtle |

Jelly comes in one of these. → jar

This creature has feathers and can fly. → bird

This animal lives in a shell. → turtle

This animal can pull wagons. → horse

If you mix water and this, you will have mud. → dirt

This color starts with the letter **p**. → purple

Discover Second Grade · 195 · © Carson-Dellosa CD-704891

195

R-Controlled Vowels

Answer the riddles below. You will need to complete the words with the correct vowel followed by r.

I am something you may use to eat. What am I? → f__or__k

My name means the opposite of tall. What am I? → sh__or__t

I can be seen high in the sky. I twinkle. What am I? → st__ar__

I am a kind of clothing a girl might wear. What am I? → sk__ir__t

I am the word for a group of cows. What am I? → h__er__d

I am a part of your body. What am I? → __ar__m

Discover Second Grade · 196 · © Carson-Dellosa CD-704891

196

Double Vowel Sounds

Usually when two vowels appear together, the first one says its name and the second one is silent.

Example: b**ea**n

Unscramble the double vowel words below. Write the correct word on the line. Then, draw and color something else that has a double vowel sound, such as seat, tear, goat, or peas.

ocat → coat   atil → tail   eetf → feet

otab → boat   apil → pail   Drawings will vary.

Discover Second Grade · 197 · © Carson-Dellosa CD-704891

197

Vowel Teams

The vowel teams **ou** and **ow** can have the same sound. You can hear it in the words **clown** and **cloud**. The vowel teams **au** and **aw** have the same sound. You hear it in the words **cause** and **law**.

Look at the pictures. Write the correct vowel team to complete each word. The first one is done for you. You may need to use a dictionary to help you with the correct spelling. In the last box, draw and color a picture of a word with a vowel team. Some examples: owl, paw, saw, and clown.

au to   h__ou__se   fl__ow__er

m__ou__th   m__ou__se   Drawings will vary.

Discover Second Grade · 198 · © Carson-Dellosa CD-704891

198

Vowel Teams

The vowel team **ea** can have a short **e** sound like in **head** or a long **e** like in **bead**. An **ea** followed by an **r** makes a sound like the one in **ear** or the one in **heard**.

Read the story. Listen for the sound ea makes in the bold words.

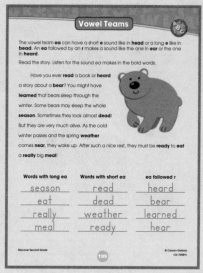

Have you ever **read** a book or **heard** a story about a **bear**? You might have **learned** that bears sleep through the winter. Some bears may sleep the whole **season**. Sometimes they look almost **dead**! But they are very much alive. As the cold winter passes and the spring **weather** comes **near**, they wake up. After such a nice rest, they must be **ready** to **eat** a **really** big **meal**!

Words with long ea	Words with short ea	ea followed r
season	read	heard
eat	dead	bear
really	weather	learned
meal	ready	hear

Discover Second Grade · 199 · © Carson-Dellosa CD-704891

199

Vowel Teams

The vowel team **ie** makes the long **e** sound as in **believe**. The team **ei** also makes the long **e** sound as in **either**. But **ei** can also make a long **a** sound as in **vein**. The teams **eigh** and **ey** also make the long **a** sound.

Circle the words with the long **a** sound.

(neighbor)   (veil)
receive   (reindeer)
(reign)   ceiling

Finish the sentences with words from the word box. Some words have the long **a** sound, and some have the long **e** sound.

| chief | sleigh | obey | weigh | thief | field | ceiling |

Eight reindeer pull Santa's → sleigh

Rules are for us to → obey

The bird got out of its cage and flew up to the → ceiling

The leader of an Indian tribe is the → chief

How much do you → weigh ?

They caught the → thief who took my bike.

Corn grows in a → field

Discover Second Grade · 200 · © Carson-Dellosa CD-704891

200

201

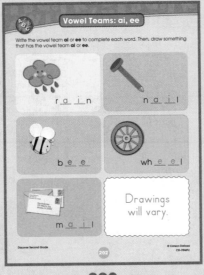

202

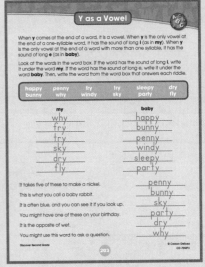

203

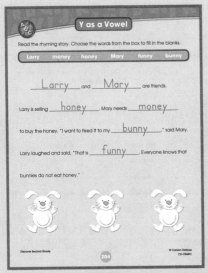

204

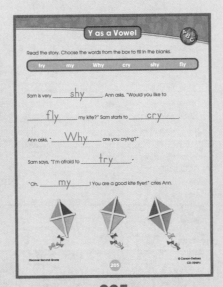

205

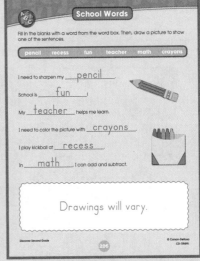

206

207

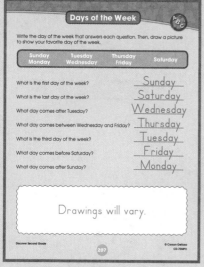

Days of the Week

Write the day of the week that answers each question. Then, draw a picture to show your favorite day of the week.

| Sunday | Tuesday | Thursday | |
| Monday | Wednesday | Friday | Saturday |

What is the first day of the week? **Sunday**

What is the last day of the week? **Saturday**

What day comes after Tuesday? **Wednesday**

What day comes between Wednesday and Friday? **Thursday**

What is the third day of the week? **Tuesday**

What day comes before Saturday? **Friday**

What day comes after Sunday? **Monday**

Drawings will vary.

208

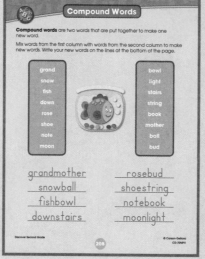

Compound Words

Compound words are two words that are put together to make one new word.

Mix words from the first column with words from the second column to make new words. Write your new words on the lines at the bottom of the page.

grand	bowl
snow	light
fish	stairs
down	string
rose	book
shoe	mother
note	ball
moon	bud

grandmother   rosebud
snowball   shoestring
fishbowl   notebook
downstairs   moonlight

209

Compound Words

Cut out the words below. Glue them together in the box to make compound words.

Can you think of any more compound words?

Compound Words

sunflower	football
mailbox	watermelon
classroom	airplane
bedroom	bodyguard

211

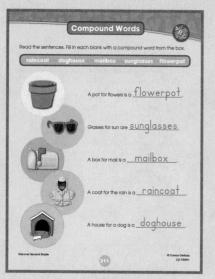

Compound Words

Read the sentences. Fill in each blank with a compound word from the box.

| raincoat | doghouse | mailbox | sunglasses | flowerpot |

A pot for flowers is a **flowerpot**

Glasses for sun are **sunglasses**

A box for mail is a **mailbox**

A coat for the rain is a **raincoat**

A house for a dog is a **doghouse**

212

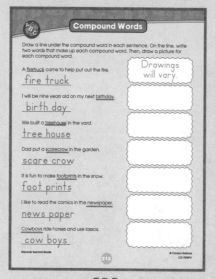

Compound Words

Draw a line under the compound word in each sentence. On the line, write two words that make up each compound word. Then, draw a picture for each compound word.

A firetruck came to help put out the fire.
fire truck

Drawings will vary.

I will be nine years old on my next birthday.
birth day

We built a treehouse in the yard.
tree house

Dad put a scarecrow in the garden.
scare crow

It is fun to make footprints in the snow.
foot prints

I like to read the comics in the newspaper.
news paper

Cowboys ride horses and use lassos.
cow boys

213

Contractions

Contractions are a short way to write two words.

Examples: **it is = it's**   **is not = isn't**   **I have = I've**

Cut out and glue each of the contractions next to the correct word pair.

Contractions

I am	I'm
it is	it's
you are	you're
we are	we're
they are	they're
she is	she's
he is	he's

Answer Key

215

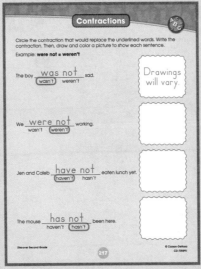

217

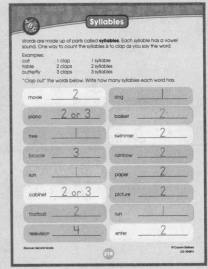

218

Page 219 (Syllables)

kitten	kit ten	harder	har der
lumber	lum ber	dirty	dir ty
batter	bat ter	sister	sis ter
winter	win ter	little	lit tle
funny	fun ny	dinner	din ner

219

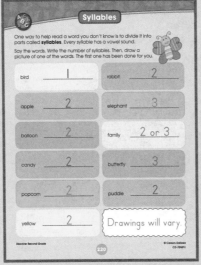

220

Page 221 (Syllables)

but ter   chat ter   mit ten
din ner   let ter   yel low
pil low   kit ten   hap py
pup py   lad der   sum mer

win dow   win ter   pic ture
mis ter   sis ter   car pet
bar ber   num ber   can dle
doc tor   pen cil   un der

221

Answer Key

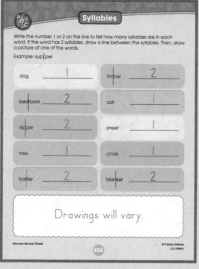

Syllables

Write the number 1 or 2 on the line to tell how many syllables are in each word. If the word has 2 syllables, draw a line between the syllables. Then, draw a picture of one of the words.

Example: sup|per

dog	1	timber	2
bedroom	2	cat	1
slipper	2	street	1
tree	1	chalk	1
batter	2	blanket	2

Drawings will vary.

222

Haiku

A **haiku** is a Japanese form of poetry.

first line: 5 syllables
second line: 7 syllables
third line: 5 syllables

Example:

The squirrel is brown.
He lives in a great big tree.
He eats nuts all day.

Write your own haiku. Draw a picture to go with it.

Answers will vary.

223

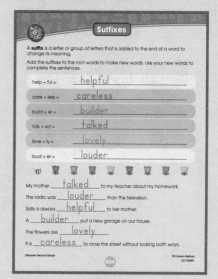

Suffixes

A **suffix** is a letter or group of letters that is added to the end of a word to change its meaning.

Add the suffixes to the root words to make new words. Use your new words to complete the sentences.

help + ful =	helpful
care + less =	careless
build + er =	builder
talk + ed =	talked
love + ly =	lovely
loud + er =	louder

My mother __talked__ to my teacher about my homework.

The radio was __louder__ than the television.

Sally is always __helpful__ to her mother.

A __builder__ put a new garage on our house.

The flowers are __lovely__.

It is __careless__ to cross the street without looking both ways.

224

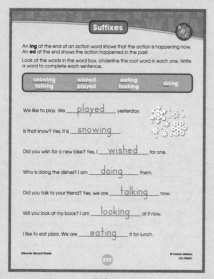

Suffixes

An **ing** at the end of an action word shows that the action is happening now. An **ed** at the end shows the action happened in the past.

Look at the words in the word box. Underline the root word in each one. Write a word to complete each sentence.

| snowing | wished | eating | doing |
| talking | played | looking | |

We like to play. We __played__ yesterday.

Is that snow? Yes, it is __snowing__.

Did you wish for a new bike? Yes, I __wished__ for one.

Who is doing the dishes? I am __doing__ them.

Did you talk to your friend? Yes, we are __talking__ now.

Will you look at my book? I am __looking__ at it now.

I like to eat pizza. We are __eating__ it for lunch.

225

Suffixes

Read the story. Underline the words that end with **est**, **ed**, or **ing**. On the lines below, write the root word for each word you underlined.

The funniest book I ever read was about a girl named Nan. Nan did everything backward. She even spelled her name backward. Nan slept during the day and played at night. She dried her hair before washing it. She turned on the light after she finished her book, which she read from the back to the front! When it rained, Nan waited until she was inside before opening her umbrella. She even walked backward. The silliest part: The only thing Nan did forward was back up!

funny	wash	open
name	turn	walk
spell	finish	silly
play	rain	
dry	wait	

226

Suffixes

Cut out the root words at the bottom of the page and glue them next to the correct word.

coming	come	rained	rain
lived	live	carried	carry
visited	visit	sitting	sit
hurried	hurry	swimming	swim
running	run	racing	race

227

Answer Key

Prefixes: The Three Rs (229)

A **prefix** is a letter or group of letters that is added to the beginning of a word to change its meaning. The prefix **re** means "again."

Read the story. Then, follow the instructions.

Kim wants to find ways she can save the Earth. She studies the "three Rs"—reduce, reuse, and recycle. **Reduce** means "to make less." Both **reuse** and **recycle** mean "to use again."

Add **re** to the beginning of each word below. Use the new words to complete the sentences.

re build | re fill
re read | re tell
re write | re run

The race was a tie, so Dawn and Kathy had to **rerun** it.
The block wall fell down, so Simon had to **rebuild** it.
The water bottle was empty, so Luna had to **refill** it.
Javier wrote a good story, but he wanted to **rewrite** it to make it better.
The teacher told a story, and students had to **retell** it.
Toni didn't understand the directions, so she had to **reread** them.

Prefixes (230)

Read the story. Change **Unlucky Sam** to **Lucky Sam** by removing the **un** prefix from the **bold** words. Write the new words in the new story. Then, draw a picture of Lucky Sam.

Unlucky Sam

Sam was **unhappy** about a lot of things in his life. His parents were **uncaring**. His teacher was **unfair**. His big sister was **unkind**. His neighbors were **unfriendly**. He was **unhealthy**, too! How could one boy be as **unlucky** as Sam?

Lucky Sam

Sam was **happy** about a lot of things in his life. His parents were **caring**. His teacher was **fair**. His big sister was **kind**. His neighbors were **friendly**. He was **healthy**, too! How could one boy be as **lucky** as Sam?

Drawings will vary.

Prefixes (231)

Read the story. Change the story by removing the prefix **re** from the **bold** words. Write the new words in the new story.

Repete is a **rewriter** who has to **redo** every story. He has to **rethink** up the ideas. He has to **rewrite** the sentences. He has to **redraw** the pictures. He even has to **retype** the pages. Who will **repay Repete** for all the work he **redoes**?

Pete is a **writer** who has to **do** every story. He has to **think** up the ideas. He has to **write** the sentences. He has to **draw** the pictures. He even has to **type** the pages. Who will **pay Pete** for all the work he **does**?

Prefixes (232)

Read each sentence. Look at the words in **bold**. Circle the prefix and write the root word on line. Then, draw a picture to show one of the sentences.

The **pre**view of the movie was funny. **view**
Please try to keep the cat **in**side the house. **side**
We will have to **re**schedule the trip. **schedule**
Are you tired of **re**runs on television? **run**
I have **out**grown my new shoes already. **grow**
You just have **mis**placed the papers. **place**
Police **en**force the laws of the city. **force**
I **dis**liked that book. **like**
Try to **en**joy yourself at the party. **joy**

Drawings will vary.

Parts of a Book (233)

A book has many parts. The **title** is the name of the book. The **author** is the person who wrote the words. The **illustrator** is the person who drew the pictures. The **table of contents** is located at the beginning to list what is in the book. The **glossary** is a little dictionary in the back to help you with unfamiliar words. Books are often divided into smaller sections of information called **chapters**.

Look at one of your books. Answer the questions about your book.

Answers will vary.

The title of my book is _____
The author is _____
The illustrator is _____

My book has a table of contents. Yes or No
My book has a glossary. Yes or No
My book is divided into chapters. Yes or No

Recalling Details: Nikki's Pets (234)

Read about Nikki's pets. Then, answer the questions.

Nikki has two cats, Tiger and Sniffer, and two dogs, Fluffy and Wiggles. Tiger is an orange cat who likes to sleep under a big tree and pretend she is a real tiger. Sniffer is a gray cat who likes to sniff the flowers in Nikki's garden. Fluffy is a gray poodle with fluffy white tufts of fur. Wiggles is a big, furry brown dog who wiggles all over when he is happy.

Which dog is brown and furry? **Wiggles**
What color is Tiger? **orange**
What kind of dog is Fluffy? **poodle**
Which cat likes to sniff flowers? **Sniffer**
Where does Tiger like to sleep? **under a big tree**
Who wiggles all over when he is happy? **Wiggles**

Answer Key

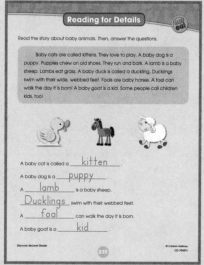

Reading for Details

Read the story about baby animals. Then, answer the questions.

Baby cats are called kittens. They love to play. A baby dog is a puppy. Puppies chew on old shoes. They run and bark. A lamb is a baby sheep. Lambs eat grass. A baby duck is called a duckling. Ducklings swim with their wide, webbed feet. Foals are baby horses. A foal can walk the day it is born! A baby goat is a kid. Some people call children kids, too!

A baby cat is called a __kitten__.

A baby dog is a __puppy__.

A __lamb__ is a baby sheep.

__Ducklings__ swim with their webbed feet.

A __foal__ can walk the day it is born.

A baby goat is a __kid__.

235

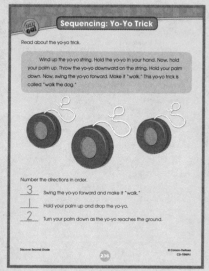

Sequencing: Yo-Yo Trick

Read about the yo-yo trick.

Wind up the yo-yo string. Hold the yo-yo in your hand. Now, hold your palm up. Throw the yo-yo downward on the string. Hold your palm down. Now, swing the yo-yo forward. Make it "walk." This yo-yo trick is called "walk the dog."

Number the directions in order.

__3__ Swing the yo-yo forward and make it "walk."

__1__ Hold your palm up and drop the yo-yo.

__2__ Turn your palm down as the yo-yo reaches the ground.

236

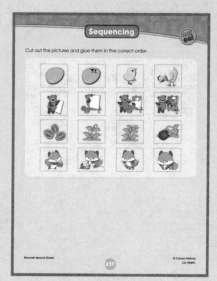

Sequencing

Cut out the pictures and glue them in the correct order.

237

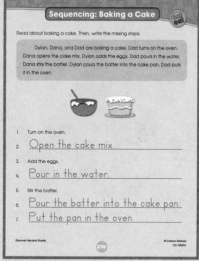

Sequencing: Baking a Cake

Read about baking a cake. Then, write the missing steps.

Dylan, Dana, and Dad are baking a cake. Dad turns on the oven. Dana opens the cake mix. Dylan adds the eggs. Dad pours in the water. Dana stirs the batter. Dylan pours the batter into the cake pan. Dad puts it in the oven.

1. Turn on the oven.
2. __Open the cake mix.__
3. Add the eggs.
4. __Pour in the water.__
5. Stir the batter.
6. __Pour the batter into the cake pan.__
7. __Put the pan in the oven.__

239

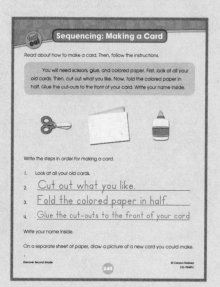

Sequencing: Making a Card

Read about how to make a card. Then, follow the instructions.

You will need scissors, glue, and colored paper. First, look at all your old cards. Then, cut out what you like. Now, fold the colored paper in half. Glue the cut-outs to the front of your card. Write your name inside.

Write the steps in order for making a card.

1. Look at all your old cards.
2. __Cut out what you like.__
3. __Fold the colored paper in half.__
4. __Glue the cut-outs to the front of your card.__

Write your name inside.

On a separate sheet of paper, draw a picture of a new card you could make.

240

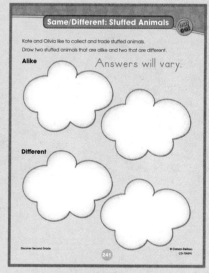

Same/Different: Stuffed Animals

Kate and Olivia like to collect and trade stuffed animals. Draw two stuffed animals that are alike and two that are different.

Alike

Answers will vary.

Different

241

Answer Key

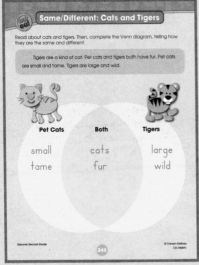

Same/Different: Cats and Tigers

Read about cats and tigers. Then, complete the Venn diagram, telling how they are the same and different.

Tigers are a kind of cat. Pet cats and tigers both have fur. Pet cats are small and tame. Tigers are large and wild.

Pet Cats	Both	Tigers
small	cats	large
tame	fur	wild

242

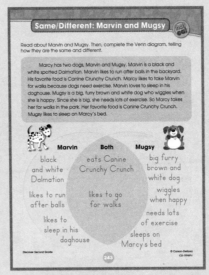

Same/Different: Marvin and Mugsy

Read about Marvin and Mugsy. Then, complete the Venn diagram, telling how they are the same and different.

Marcy has two dogs, Marvin and Mugsy. Marvin is a black and white spotted Dalmatian. Marvin likes to run after balls in the backyard. His favorite food is Canine Crunchy Crunch. Marcy likes to take Marvin for walks because dogs need exercise. Mugsy loves to sleep in his doghouse. Mugsy is a big, furry brown and white dog who wiggles when she is happy. Since she is big, she needs lots of exercise. So Marcy takes her for walks in the park. Her favorite food is Canine Crunchy Crunch. Mugsy likes to sleep on Marcy's bed.

Marvin: black and white Dalmation, likes to run after balls, likes to sleep in his doghouse

Both: eats Canine Crunchy Crunch, likes to go for walks

Mugsy: big furry brown and white dog, wiggles when happy, needs lots of exercise, sleeps on Marcy's bed

243

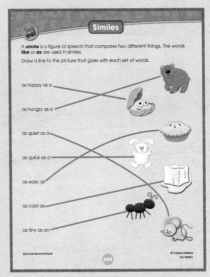

Similes

A **simile** is a figure of speech that compares two different things. The words **like** or **as** are used in similes.

Draw a line to the picture that goes with each set of words.

as happy as a
as hungry as a
as quiet as a
as quick as a
as easy as
as cold as
as tiny as an

244

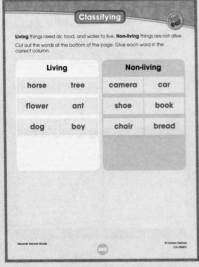

Classifying

Living things need air, food, and water to live. **Non-living** things are not alive.

Cut out the words at the bottom of the page. Glue each word in the correct column.

Living		Non-living	
horse	tree	camera	car
flower	ant	shoe	book
dog	boy	chair	bread

245

Classifying

Read the sentences. Write the words from the word box where they belong.

bush rocket cake thunder bicycle Danger
airplane wind candy rain car grass
Stop truck Poison flower pie bird

These things taste sweet.
cake candy pie

These things come when it storms.
wind thunder rain

These things have wheels.
car truck bicycle

These are words you see on signs.
Stop Poison Danger

These things can fly.
rocket bird airplane

These things grow in the ground.
flower grass bush

247

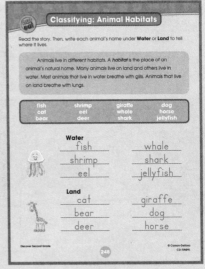

Classifying: Animal Habitats

Read the story. Then, write each animal's name under **Water** or **Land** to tell where it lives.

Animals live in different habitats. A *habitat* is the place of an animal's natural home. Many animals live on land and others live in water. Most animals that live in water breathe with gills. Animals that live on land breathe with lungs.

fish shrimp giraffe dog
cat eel whale horse
bear deer shark jellyfish

Water
fish whale
shrimp shark
eel jellyfish

Land
cat giraffe
bear dog
deer horse

248

Answer Key

Comprehension: Playful Cats

Read about cats. Then, follow the instructions.

Cats make good pets. They like to play. They like to jump. They like to run. Do you?

Cats make good __pets__.

Write three things cats like to do.
__play__
__jump__
__run__

Think of a good name for a cat. Write it on the line and then draw a picture of a cat.
__Answers will vary.__

Drawings will vary.

249

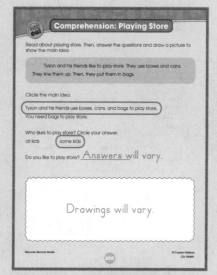

Comprehension: Playing Store

Read about playing store. Then, answer the questions and draw a picture to show the main idea.

Tyson and his friends like to play store. They use boxes and cans. They line them up. Then, they put them in bags.

Circle the main idea.
(Tyson and his friends use boxes, cans, and bags to play store.)
You need bags to play store.

Who likes to play store? Circle your answer.
all kids   (some kids)

Do you like to play store? __Answers will vary.__

Drawings will vary.

250

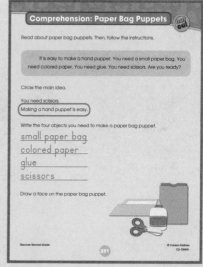

Comprehension: Paper Bag Puppets

Read about paper bag puppets. Then, follow the instructions.

It is easy to make a hand puppet. You need a small paper bag. You need colored paper. You need glue. You need scissors. Are you ready?

Circle the main idea.
You need scissors.
(Making a hand puppet is easy.)

Write the four objects you need to make a paper bag puppet.
__small paper bag__
__colored paper__
__glue__
__scissors__

Draw a face on the paper bag puppet.

251

Comprehension: A Winter Story

Read about winter. Then, follow the instructions.

It is cold in winter. Most kids like to play outdoors. Some kids make a snowman. Some kids skate. What do you do in winter?

Circle the main idea.
Snow falls in winter.
(In winter, there are many things to do outside.)

Write two things about winter weather.
__Answers will vary.__

Write what you like to do in winter. Then, draw a picture.
__Answers will vary.__

Drawings will vary.

252

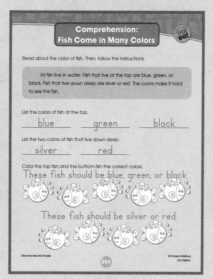

Comprehension: Fish Come in Many Colors

Read about the color of fish. Then, follow the instructions.

All fish live in water. Fish that live at the top are blue, green, or black. Fish that live down deep are silver or red. The colors make it hard to see the fish.

List the colors of fish at the top.
__blue__   __green__   __black__

List the two colors of fish that live down deep.
__silver__   __red__

Color the top fish and the bottom fish the correct colors.
These fish should be blue, green, or black.

These fish should be silver or red.

253

Predicting Outcomes

Complete the story. Then, draw pictures to match the four parts.
__Answers will vary.__

Sylvia and Marge are flying a kite.

Drawings will vary.

Beginning   **Middle**

The kite gets stuck in a tree.

Middle   **End**

254

Discover Second Grade

370

© Carson-Dellosa
CD-704891

Predicting Outcomes

Draw pictures to create your own story in the squares. Show the beginning, middle, and end in the appropriate boxes.

Drawings will vary.

Beginning (Setting)

Middle (Problem)

Middle (Problem)

End (Solution)

Discover Second Grade

© Carson-Dellosa
CD-704891

255

255

Fact and Opinion: Henrietta the Humpback

Read the story. Then, follow the instructions.

My name is Henrietta, and I am a humpback whale. I live in cold seas in the summer and warm seas in the winter. My long flippers are used to move forward and backward. I like to eat fish. Sometimes, I show off by leaping out of the water. Would you like to be a humpback whale?

Write **F** next to each fact and **O** next to each opinion.

O Being a humpback whale is fun.

F Humpback whales live in cold seas during the summer.

O Whales are fun to watch.

F Humpback whales use their flippers to move forward and backward.

O Henrietta is a great name for a whale.

O Leaping out of the water would be hard.

F Humpback whales like to eat fish.

F Humpback whales show off by leaping out of the water.

Discover Second Grade

256

© Carson-Dellosa
CD-704891

256

Making Inferences: Ryan's Globe

Read about Ryan's globe. Then, follow the instructions.

Ryan got a new globe. He wanted to place it where it would be safe. He asked his dad to put it up high. Where can his dad put the globe?

Write where Ryan's dad can put the globe. Answers may include:
on top of the refrigerator;
on a closet shelf

Draw a place Ryan's dad can put the globe.

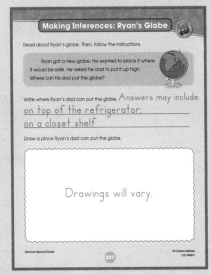

Drawings will vary.

Discover Second Grade

257

© Carson-Dellosa
CD-704891

257

Making Inferences: Visualizing

Read the story about Melinda. Then, draw pictures that describe each part of the story.

Beginning: It was Halloween. Melinda's costume was a black cat with super-duper-polka-dot sunglasses.

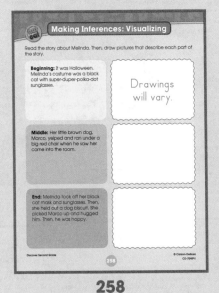

Drawings will vary.

Middle: Her little brown dog, Marco, yelped and ran under a big red chair when he saw her come into the room.

End: Melinda took off her black cat mask and sunglasses. Then, she held out a dog biscuit. She picked Marco up and hugged him. Then, he was happy.

Discover Second Grade

258

© Carson-Dellosa
CD-704891

258

Making Inferences: Point of View

Juniper has three problems to solve. She needs your help. Read each problem. Write what you think she should do.

Juniper is watching her favorite TV show when the power goes out.

Answers will vary.

Juniper is riding her bike to school when the front tire goes flat.

Juniper loses her father while shopping in the supermarket.

Discover Second Grade

259

© Carson-Dellosa
CD-704891

259

Making Inferences: Sequencing

Draw three pictures to tell a story about each topic.

Feeding a pet	Playing with a friend
Drawings will vary.	
Beginning	Beginning
Middle	Middle
End	End

Discover Second Grade

260

© Carson-Dellosa
CD-704891

260

Answer Key

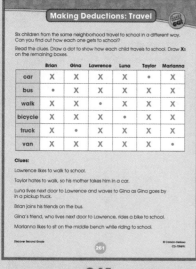

Making Deductions: Travel

Six children from the same neighborhood travel to school in a different way. Can you find out how each one gets to school?

Read the clues. Draw a dot to show how each child travels to school. Draw **X**s on the remaining boxes.

	Brian	Gina	Lawrence	Luna	Taylor	Marianna
car	X	X	X	X	•	X
bus	•	X	X	X	X	X
walk	X	X	•	X	X	X
bicycle	X	X	X	•	X	X
truck	X	•	X	X	X	X
van	X	X	X	X	X	•

Clues:

Lawrence likes to walk to school.

Taylor hates to walk, so his mother takes him in a car.

Luna lives next door to Lawrence and waves to Gina as Gina goes by in a pickup truck.

Brian joins his friends on the bus.

Gina's friend, who lives next door to Lawrence, rides a bike to school.

Marianna likes to sit on the middle bench while riding to school.

Discover Second Grade

261

© Carson-Dellosa
CD-704891

261

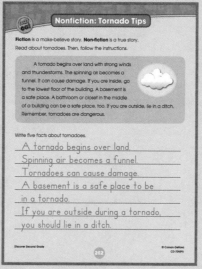

Nonfiction: Tornado Tips

Fiction is a make-believe story. **Non-fiction** is a true story.
Read about tornadoes. Then, follow the instructions.

A tornado begins over land with strong winds and thunderstorms. The spinning air becomes a funnel. It can cause damage. If you are inside, go to the lowest floor of the building. A basement is a safe place. A bathroom or closet in the middle of a building can be a safe place, too. If you are outside, lie in a ditch. Remember, tornadoes are dangerous.

Write five facts about tornadoes.

A tornado begins over land.
Spinning air becomes a funnel.
Tornadoes can cause damage.
A basement is a safe place to be
in a tornado.
If you are outside during a tornado,
you should lie in a ditch.

Discover Second Grade

262

© Carson-Dellosa
CD-704891

262

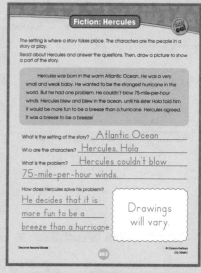

Fiction: Hercules

The setting is where a story takes place. The characters are the people in a story or play.

Read about Hercules and answer the questions. Then, draw a picture to show a part of the story.

Hercules was born in the warm Atlantic Ocean. He was a very small and weak baby. He wanted to be the strongest hurricane in the world. But he had one problem. He couldn't blow 75-mile-per-hour winds. Hercules blew and blew in the ocean, until his sister Hola told him it would be more fun to be a breeze than a hurricane. Hercules agreed. It was a breeze to be a breeze!

What is the setting of the story? _Atlantic Ocean_

Who are the characters? _Hercules, Hola_

What is the problem? _Hercules couldn't blow 75-mile-per-hour winds._

How does Hercules solve his problem?
He decides that it is more fun to be a breeze than a hurricane.

Drawings will vary.

Discover Second Grade

263

© Carson-Dellosa
CD-704891

263

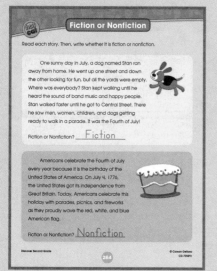

Fiction or Nonfiction

Read each story. Then, write whether it is fiction or nonfiction.

One sunny day in July, a dog named Stan ran away from home. He went up one street and down the other looking for fun, but all the yards were empty. Where was everybody? Stan kept walking until he heard the sound of band music and happy people. Stan walked faster until he got to Central Street. There he saw men, women, children, and dogs getting ready to walk in a parade. It was the Fourth of July!

Fiction or Nonfiction? _Fiction_

Americans celebrate the Fourth of July every year because it is the birthday of the United States of America. On July 4, 1776, the United States got its independence from Great Britain. Today, Americans celebrate this holiday with parades, picnics, and fireworks as they proudly wave the red, white, and blue American flag.

Fiction or Nonfiction? _Nonfiction_

Discover Second Grade

264

© Carson-Dellosa
CD-704891

264

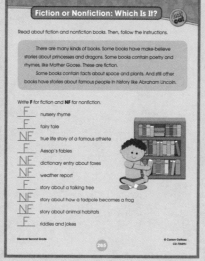

Fiction or Nonfiction: Which Is It?

Read about fiction and nonfiction books. Then, follow the instructions.

There are many kinds of books. Some books have make-believe stories about princesses and dragons. Some books contain poetry and rhymes, like Mother Goose. These are fiction.

Some books contain facts about space and plants. And still other books have stories about famous people in history like Abraham Lincoln.

Write **F** for fiction and **NF** for nonfiction.

_F_ nursery rhyme
_F_ fairy tale
_NF_ true life story of a famous athlete
_F_ Aesop's fables
_NF_ dictionary entry about foxes
_NF_ weather report
_F_ story about a talking tree
_NF_ story about how a tadpole becomes a frog
_NF_ story about animal habitats
_F_ riddles and jokes

Discover Second Grade

265

© Carson-Dellosa
CD-704891

265

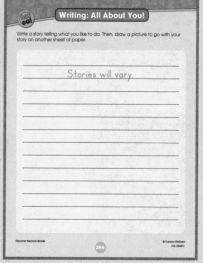

Writing: All About You!

Write a story telling what you like to do. Then, draw a picture to go with your story on another sheet of paper.

Stories will vary.

Discover Second Grade

266

© Carson-Dellosa
CD-704891

266

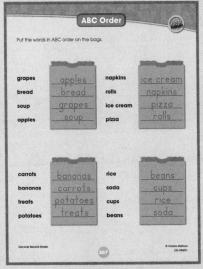

267

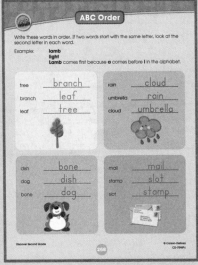

268

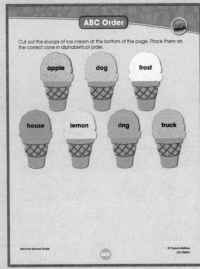

269

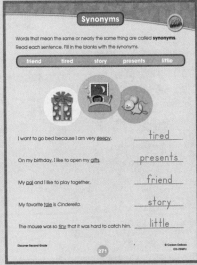

271

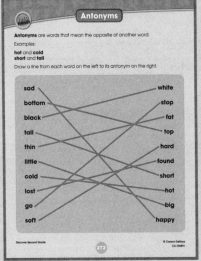

272

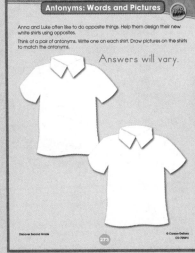

273

Answer Key

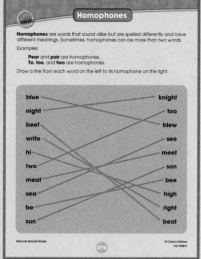

274

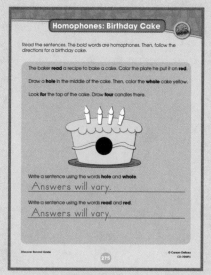

275

276

277

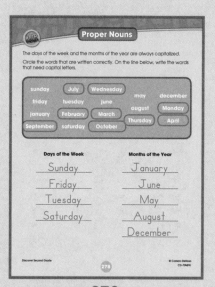

278

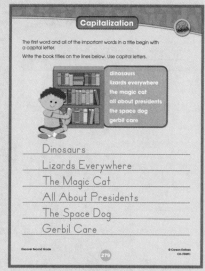

279

280

Plurals

Plurals are words that mean more than one. To make a word plural, you add an **s** or **es**. In some words ending in **y**, the **y** changes to an **i** before **es**. For example, **baby** changes to **babies**.

Look at the following lists of plural words. Next to each, write the word that means one. Then, draw a picture to show one of the words.

dresses	dress	pencils	pencil
bushes	bush	candles	candy
foxes	fox	wishes	wish
chairs	chair	boxes	box
shoes	shoe	ladies	lady
stories	story	bunnies	bunny
puppies	puppy	desks	desk

Drawings will vary.

281

Pronouns

Pronouns are words that can be used instead of nouns. **She**, **he**, **it**, and **they** are pronouns.

Read the sentence. Then, write the sentence again, using **she**, **he**, **it**, or **they** in the blank. Draw a picture to show one of the sentences.

Dan likes funny jokes. ___He___ likes funny jokes.

Peg and Sam went to the zoo. ___They___ went to the zoo.

My mom's car was covered in snow. ___It___ was covered in snow.

Sara is a very good dancer. ___She___ is a very good dancer.

Fred and Ted are twins. ___They___ are twins.

Drawings will vary.

282

Subjects

The **subject** of a sentence is the person, place, or thing the sentence is about.

Underline the subject in each sentence. Then, draw pictures to show the sentences.

Example: Mom read a book.
  (Think: Who is the sentence about? Mom)

The bird flew away.

The kite was high in the air.

The children played a game.

The books fell down.

The monkey climbed a tree.

Drawings will vary.

283

Compound Subjects

Two similar sentences can be joined into one sentence if the predicate is the same. A **compound subject** is made up of two subjects joined together by a conjunction like **and**.

Example:

Jamie can sing.
Sandy can sing.
Jamie **and** Sandy can sing.

Combine the sentences. Write the new sentence on the line.

The cats are my pets.
The dogs are my pets.

The cats and dogs are my pets.

Chairs are in the store.
Tables are in the store.

Chairs and tables are in the store.

Jen is wearing a red dress.
Alice is wearing a red dress.

Jen and Alice are wearing red dresses

284

Verbs

A **verb** is the action word in a sentence. Verbs tell what something does or that something exists.

Example:

Run, **sleep**, and **jump** are verbs.

Circle the verbs in the sentences below. Then, draw a picture to show one of the sentences.

We play baseball every day.

Susan pitches the ball very well.

Mike swings the bat harder than anyone.

Chris slides into home base.

Laura hit a home run.

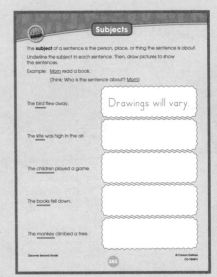

Drawings will vary.

285

Verbs

We use verbs to tell when something happens. Sometimes, we add an **ed** to verbs that tell us if something has already happened.

Example:

Today, we will **play**. Yesterday, we **played**.

Write the correct verb in the blank. Then, draw a picture to show one of the sentences.

Today, I will ___wash___ my dog, Fritz.
  wash   washed

Last week, Fritz ___cried___ when we said, "Bath time, Fritz!"
  cry   cried

My sister likes to ___help___ wash Fritz.
  help   helped

One time she ___cleaned___ Fritz by herself.
  clean   cleaned

Fritz will ___look___ a lot better after his bath.
  look   looked

Drawings will vary.

Predicates

The **predicate** is the part of the sentence that tells about the action.

Circle the predicate in each sentence. Then, draw a picture to show one of the sentences.

Example: The boys (ran) on the playground.
Think: The boys did what?

The woman (painted) a picture.

The puppy (chases) his ball.

The students (went) to school.

Butterflies (fly) in the air.

The baby (wants) a drink.

Drawings will vary.

286

Compound Predicates

A **compound predicate** is made by joining two sentences that have the same subject. The predicates are usually joined together by the word **and**.

Example:

Tom can jump.
Tom can run.
Tom can run **and** jump.

Combine the sentences. Write the new sentence on the line.

The dog can roll over.
The dog can bark.

The dog can roll over and bark.

Sam is drawing.
Sam is coloring.

Sam is drawing and coloring.

Tara is tall.
Tara is smart.

Tara is tall and smart.

287

Subjects and Predicates

The **subject** of the sentence is the person, place, or thing the sentence is about. The **predicate** is the part of the sentence that describes the subject or tells what the subject does.

Draw a line between the subject and the predicate. Underline the noun in the subject and circle the verb in the predicate. Then, draw a picture of one of the sentences.

Example: The furry <u>cat</u> | (ate) the food.

<u>Mandy</u> | (walks) to school.

The <u>bus</u> | (drove) the children.

The school <u>bell</u> | (rang) very loudly.

The <u>teacher</u> | (spoke) to the students.

The <u>girls</u> | (opened) their books.

Drawings will vary.

288

Compound Subjects and Predicates

The following sentences have either a compound subject or a compound predicate.

If the sentence has a compound subject (more than one thing doing the action), **underline** the subject. If it has a compound predicate (more than one action), **circle** the predicate.

Examples:
<u>Bats and owls</u> like the night.
The fox (slinks and spies).

Ducks (swim and quack).

Sloths (climb and sleep) in trees.

<u>Bees and mosquitos</u> fly.

Snakes (slither and hiss).

<u>Frogs and penguins</u> swim.

289

Adjectives

Adjectives are words tell more about a person, place, or thing.

Examples: Cold, dark, fuzzy

Circle the adjectives in the sentences. Then, draw a picture to show one of the sentences.

The (juicy) apple is on the plate.

The (furry) dog is eating a bone.

It was a (sunny) day.

The (cute) kitten jumps on the couch.

The sky was (dark).

Drawings will vary.

290

Articles

Articles are small words that help us to better understand nouns. **A** and **an** are articles. We use **an** before a word that begins with a vowel. We use **a** before a word that begins with a consonant.

Example: We looked in **a** nest. It had **an** eagle in it.

Read the sentences. Write **a** or **an** in the blank.

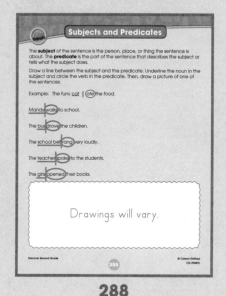

I found __a__ book.

It had a story about __an__ ant in it.

In the story, __a__ lion gave three wishes to __an__ ant.

The ant's first wish was to ride __a__ zebra.

The second wish was to ride __a__ horse.

The last wish was __a__ wish for three more wishes.

291

Answer Key

Sentences and Non-Sentences

A **sentence** tells a complete idea. It has a noun and a verb. It begins with a capital letter and has punctuation at the end.

Circle the group of words if it is a sentence. Then, draw a picture to show one of the sentences.

(Grass is a green plant.)

Mowing the lawn.

(Grass grows in fields and lawns.)

(Sheep, cows, and horses eat grass.)

We like to play in.

A picnic on the grass.

Plant flowers around.

Drawings will vary.

292

Statements

Statements are sentences that tell us something. They begin with a capital letter and end with a period.

Write the statements on the lines below. Begin each sentence with a capital letter and end it with a period. Then, draw a picture to show one of the sentences.

we like to ride our bikes
We like to ride our bikes.

we go down the hill very fast
We go down the hill very fast.

we keep our bikes shiny and clean
We keep our bikes shiny and clean.

we know how to change the tires
We know how to change the tires.

Drawings will vary.

293

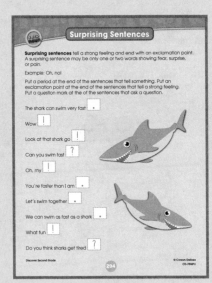

Surprising Sentences

Surprising sentences tell a strong feeling and end with an exclamation point. A surprising sentence may be only one or two words showing fear, surprise, or pain.

Example: Oh, no!

Put a period at the end of the sentences that tell something. Put an exclamation point at the end of the sentences that tell a strong feeling. Put a question mark at the of the sentences that ask a question.

The shark can swim very fast [.]

Wow [!]

Look at that shark go [.]

Can you swim fast [?]

Oh, my [!]

You're faster than I am [.]

Let's swim together [!]

We can swim as fast as a shark [.]

What fun [!]

Do you think sharks get tired [?]

294

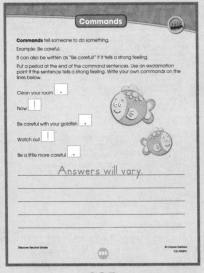

Commands

Commands tell someone to do something.

Example: Be careful.

It can also be written as "Be careful!" if it tells a strong feeling.

Put a period at the end of the command sentences. Use an exclamation point if the sentence tells a strong feeling. Write your own commands on the lines below.

Clean your room [.]

Now [!]

Be careful with your goldfish [.]

Watch out [!]

Be a little more careful [.]

Answers will vary.

295

Questions

Questions are sentences that ask something. They begin with a capital letter and end with a question mark.

Write the questions on the lines below. Begin each sentence with a capital letter and end it with a question mark.

will you be my friend
Will you be my friend?

what is your name
What is your name?

are you eight years old
Are you eight years old?

do you like rainbows
Do you like rainbows?

296

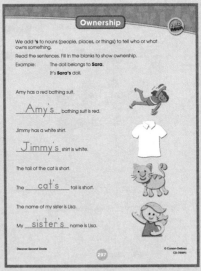

Ownership

We add **'s** to nouns (people, places, or things) to tell who or what owns something.

Read the sentences. Fill in the blanks to show ownership.

Example: The doll belongs to **Sara**.
It's **Sara's** doll.

Amy has a red bathing suit.

___Amy's___ bathing suit is red.

Jimmy has a white shirt.

___Jimmy's___ shirt is white.

The tail of the cat is short.

The ___cat's___ tail is short.

The name of my sister is Lisa.

My ___sister's___ name is Lisa.

297

Answer Key

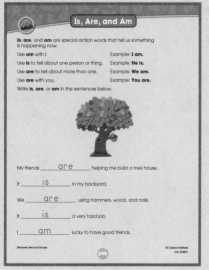

298

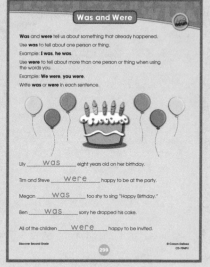

299

300

301

302

303

Answer Key

304

verb
noun

Leave, Leaves, and Left

We use **leave** and **leaves** to tell about now. We use **left** to tell about what already happened.

Write **leave**, **leaves**, or **left** in the sentences below.

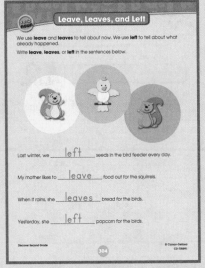

Last winter, we __left__ seeds in the bird feeder every day.

My mother likes to __leave__ food out for the squirrels.

When it rains, she __leaves__ bread for the birds.

Yesterday, she __left__ popcorn for the birds.

Discover Second Grade   304   © Carson-Dellosa
CD-704891

305

Learning Dictionary Skills

A dictionary is a book that gives the meanings of words. It also tells how words sound. Words in a dictionary are in ABC order. That makes them easier to find.

Look at this page from a dictionary. Then, answer the questions and color the pictures.

baby
a very young child

band
a group of people who play music

bank
a place where money is kept

bark
the sound a dog makes

berry
a small, juicy fruit

board
a flat piece of wood

What is a small, juicy fruit?   __berry__

What is a group of people who play music?   __band__

What is the name of a very young child?   __baby__

What is a flat piece of wood called?   __board__

Discover Second Grade   305   © Carson-Dellosa
CD-704891

306

Learning Dictionary Skills

Look at this page from a dictionary. Then, answer the questions and color the pictures.

safe: a metal box
sea: a body of water
seed: the beginning of a plant
sheep: an animal that has wool
store: a place where items are sold
skate: a shoe with wheels or a blade on it
snowstorm: a time when much snow falls
squirrel: a small animal with a bushy tail
stone: a small rock

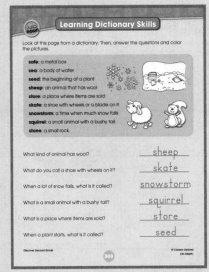

What kind of animal has wool?   __sheep__

What do you call a shoe with wheels on it?   __skate__

When a lot of snow falls, what is it called?   __snowstorm__

What is a small animal with a bushy tail?   __squirrel__

What is a place where items are sold?   __store__

When a plant starts, what is it called?   __seed__

Discover Second Grade   306   © Carson-Dellosa
CD-704891

307

Learning Dictionary Skills

Look at this page from a dictionary. Then, answer the questions and draw something that could come after **tiger** in the dictionary.

table: furniture with legs and a flat top
teacher: a person who teaches lessons
telephone: a device that sends and receives sounds
ticket: a paper slip or card that allows someone to enter an event
tiger: an animal with stripes

Who is a person who teaches lessons?   __teacher__

What is the name of an animal with stripes?   __tiger__

What is a piece of furniture with legs and a flat top?   __table__

What is the definition of a ticket?

__a paper slip or card that allows someone to enter an event__

What is a device that sends and receives sounds?

__telephone__   Drawings will vary.

Discover Second Grade   307   © Carson-Dellosa
CD-704891

308

Learning Dictionary Skills

The guide words at the top of a page in a dictionary tell you what the first and last words on the page will be. Only words that come in ABC order between those two words will be on that page. Guide words help you find the page you need to look up a word.

Write each word from the box in ABC order between each pair of guide words.

faint	far	fence	feed	farmer
fan	feet	farm	family	face

face   **fence**

__face__   __farm__

__faint__   __farmer__

__family__   __feed__

__fan__   __feet__

__far__   __fence__

Discover Second Grade   308   © Carson-Dellosa
CD-704891

309

Learning Dictionary Skills

Create your own dictionary page. Include guide words at the top. Write the words with their meanings in ABC order. Then, draw and color a picture of one of the words.

Answers will vary.

guide word   guide word

word

word

word   word

word   Drawings will vary.

Discover Second Grade   309   © Carson-Dellosa
CD-704891

Answer Key

Short a Words: Rhyming Words

Short a is the sound you hear in the word **math**.

Use the **short a** words in the box to write rhyming words. Then, draw a picture of one of the words.

| lamp | math | can | stamp | bat | fan | Dan |
| path | fat | | | cat | van | sat |

Write four words that rhyme with **mat**.

fat   bat   cat   sat

Write two words that rhyme with **bath**.

path   math

Write two words that rhyme with **damp**.

lamp   stamp

Write four words that rhyme with **pan**.

can
fan
van
Dan

Drawings will vary.

310

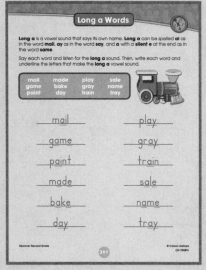

Long a Words

Long a is a vowel sound that says its own name. **Long a** can be spelled **ai** as in the word **mail**, **ay** as in the word **say**, and **a** with a **silent e** at the end as in the word **same**.

Say each word and listen for the **long a** sound. Then, write each word and underline the letters that make the **long a** vowel sound.

mail	made	play	sale
game	bake	gray	name
paint	day	train	tray

mail   play
game   gray
paint   train
made   sale
bake   name
day   tray

311

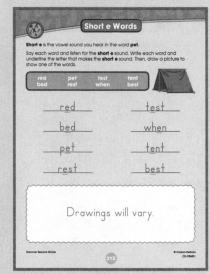

Short e Words

Short e is the vowel sound you hear in the word **pet**.

Say each word and listen for the **short e** sound. Write each word and underline the letter that makes the **short e** sound. Then, draw a picture to show one of the words.

| red | pet | test | tent |
| bed | rest | when | best |

red   test
bed   when
pet   tent
rest   best

Drawings will vary.

312

Long e Words: Rhyming Words

Long e is the vowel sound you hear in the word **meet**.

Use the **long e** words in the box to write rhyming words. Then, draw a picture to show one of the words.

| street | mean | deal | neat | clean | meal |
| keep | feet | beast | sleep | treat | feast |

Write the words that rhyme with **beat**.

street   feet   neat   treat

Write the words that rhyme with **deep**.

keep   sleep

Write the words that rhyme with **feel**.

deal   meal

Write the words that rhyme with **bean**.

mean   clean

Write the words that rhyme with **least**.

beast   feast

Drawings will vary.

313

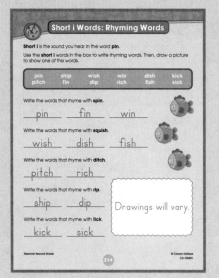

Short i Words: Rhyming Words

Short i is the sound you hear in the word **pin**.

Use the **short i** words in the box to write rhyming words. Then, draw a picture to show one of the words.

| pin | ship | wish | win | dish | kick |
| pitch | fin | dip | rich | fish | sick |

Write the words that rhyme with **spin**.

pin   fin   win

Write the words that rhyme with **squish**.

wish   dish   fish

Write the words that rhyme with **ditch**.

pitch   rich

Write the words that rhyme with **rip**.

ship   dip

Write the words that rhyme with **lick**.

kick   sick

Drawings will vary.

314

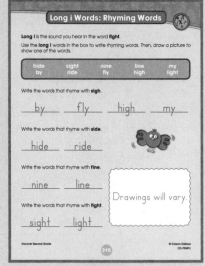

Long i Words: Rhyming Words

Long i is the sound you hear in the word **fight**.

Use the **long i** words in the box to write rhyming words. Then, draw a picture to show one of the words.

| hide | sight | nine | line | my |
| by | ride | fly | high | light |

Write the words that rhyme with **sigh**.

by   fly   high   my

Write the words that rhyme with **side**.

hide   ride

Write the words that rhyme with **fine**.

nine   line

Write the words that rhyme with **fight**.

sight   light

Drawings will vary.

315

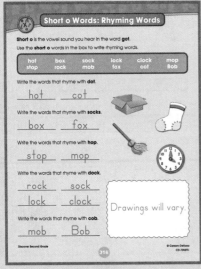

316

Short o Words: Rhyming Words

Short **o** is the vowel sound you hear in the word **got**.
Use the **short o** words in the box to write rhyming words.

| hot | box | sock | lock | clock | mop |
| stop | rock | mob | fox | cot | Bob |

Write the words that rhyme with **dot**.
hot   cot

Write the words that rhyme with **socks**.
box   fox

Write the words that rhyme with **hop**.
stop   mop

Write the words that rhyme with **dock**.
rock   sock
lock   clock

Write the words that rhyme with **cob**.
mob   Bob

Drawings will vary.

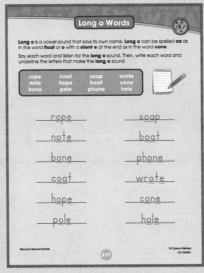

317

Long o Words

rope   soap
note   boat
bone   phone
coat   wrote
hope   cone
pole   hole

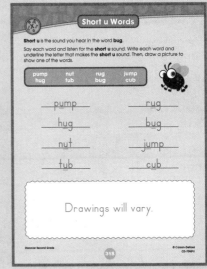

318

Short u Words

pump   rug
hug   bug
nut   jump
tub   cub

Drawings will vary.

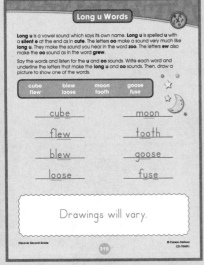

319

Long u Words

cube   moon
flew   tooth
blew   goose
loose   fuse

Drawings will vary.

320

Family Words

Example:
funny tall — My aunt is tall and funny
happy smiling — My grandmother is happy and smiling
hot tired — My uncle is hot and tired
thirsty hungry — My little brother is thirsty and hungry

321

Family Words: Joining Words

but — My aunt lives far away, but she calls me often.
and — My sister had a birthday, and she got a new bike.
or — We can play outside, or we can play inside.

Location Words

Use one of the location words from the box to complete each sentence. Then, color the pictures.

| between | around | inside | outside | beside | across |

Example:
She will hide ___under___ the basket.

In the summer, we like to play ___outside___.

She can swim ___across___ the pool.

Put the bird ___inside___ its cage so it won't fly away.

Sit ___between___ Bill and me so we can all work together.

Your picture is right ___beside___ mine on the wall.

The bunny hopped ___around___ the park.

Discover Second Grade

322

© Carson-Dellosa
CD-704891

322

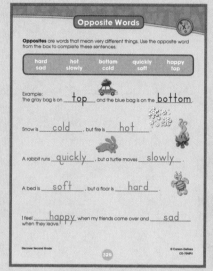

Opposite Words

Opposites are words that mean very different things. Use the opposite word from the box to complete these sentences.

| hard | hot | bottom | quickly | happy |
| sad | slowly | cold | soft | top |

Example:
The gray bag is on ___top___ and the blue bag is on the ___bottom___.

Snow is ___cold___, but fire is ___hot___.

A rabbit runs ___quickly___, but a turtle moves ___slowly___.

A bed is ___soft___, but a floor is ___hard___.

I feel ___happy___ when my friends come over and ___sad___ when they leave.

Discover Second Grade

329

© Carson-Dellosa
CD-704891

329

Time Words

The time between breakfast and lunch is **morning**.
The time between lunch and dinner is **afternoon**.
The time between dinner and bedtime is **evening**.
Write a time word from the box to complete each sentence. Use each word only once.

| afternoon | evening | morning | today | tomorrow |

What did you eat for breakfast this ___morning___ ?

We came home from school in the ___afternoon___.

I help wash the dinner dishes in the ___evening___.

I feel a little tired ___today___.

If I rest tonight, I will feel better ___tomorrow___

Discover Second Grade

330

© Carson-Dellosa
CD-704891

330

Notes

cover Second Grade

© Carson-Dellosa
CD-704891